Renaissance Patterns Volume 1

German Modelbücher 1524–1556

A Compilation of Eight German Needlework and Weaving Pattern Books

Copyright © 2018 Marion McNealy
All rights reserved. This book or any portion thereof may not be reproduced or used in any manner whatsoever without the express written permission of the publisher except for the use of brief quotations in a book review.

While the images in this book have all been placed in the public domain by their respective museums, the work to analyze and compile them and prepare them for publication is not in the public domain. If you wish to use any of these images, please use the information provided in the book to go to the museum website and download a copy for your own use.

Published by Nadel und Faden Press, LLC Kennewick, Washington, USA
www.nadelundfadenpress.com

Publisher's Cataloging-in-Publication Data
provided by Five Rainbows Cataloging Services

Names: McNealy, Marion, author.
Title: German Modelbücher 1524 – 1556: a compilation of eight German needlework and weaving pattern books/Marion McNealy.
Description: Kennewick, WA: Nadel und Faden Press, 2018. | Series: Renaissance patterns, vol. 1.
Identifiers: ISBN 978-0-9985977-2-0 (pbk.).
Subjects: LCSH: Embroidery--Patterns. | Needlework--Patterns. | Hand weaving--Patterns. | Embroidery--Germany--16th century. | Pattern books--Germany--16th century. | BISAC: CRAFTS & HOBBIES/Fiber Arts & Textiles. | HISTORY/Europe/Germany.
Classification: LCC NK8809.3 .M36 2018 (print) | LCC NK8809.3 (ebook) | DDC 746.4--dc23.
Library of Congress Control Number: 2018911783
ISBN: 0998597724
ISBN-13: 978-0998597720

Design & Layout: Tina Vadász-Hain, www.expresso-grafik.de

Cover Image: Hoffman 1556 f.1r

Table of Contents

Acknowledgments — 4
Preface — 5
Introduction — 7
   The Modelbücher — 7
   The Manuscripts — 9
Woven Bands and Fabric — 27
Embroidery and Needlework — 38
   Pleated Shirts — 39
   Goldwork and Pearls — 42
   Satin Stitch with Gold Work — 46
   Cord Work — 47
   Glattstich – Satin Stitch — 48
   Weiss Arbeit – White Work — 50
   Spanish Stitch – Double Running, and Cross Stitch — 53
   Metalwork — 55
Freestyle Patterns
   Plates 1 – 124 — 57
Charted Patterns
   Plates 125 – 200 — 183

Acknowledgments

This book would not be possible without the invaluable help of many people. First off, sincere thanks to the many museums who have put their photos out in to the public domain. Without them, this book would not be possible. Thank you to Katherine Barich for the translation work, to Robin Berry for the encouragement, to Lara Baker-Olin for help with weaving structures, and to Anne Marie Decker for the pep talk on the phone. To my son who always had an encouraging word about the book when I was despairing over various book-related things. To Tina, who had great advice on how to clean up the original photos and made the book look great. Special thanks to F, S, and HS for always providing the inspiration, strength, and energy when I needed it.

And, finally, to the woman with whom I once got into an argument about how the charted patterns in a *modelbuch* could be used. She insisted that they could only be used for cross stitch; I insisted that they could be used for anything, from embroidery to weaving. However, I couldn't prove it at the time, because of the lack of museum collections online. Thankfully, this has now changed, and I hope this work proves my point. CG, this book is my response to your "Prove it!" Although it's about 11 years too late and I have no idea where in the world you currently are located. Thank you for giving me the challenge which was the inspiration for this work.

Marion McNealy, October 2018

Preface

For several years I've really longed for a good 16th century German embroidery and weaving pattern reference book. I wanted a book that I could look through when I saw a design in a painting, to see if the same design, or a very similar one, could be found in a 16th c. pattern book. I also wanted it to be a book that I could use when planning projects around a specific date, say "The year is 1532, what designs are available to use?"

While there are many extant pattern books which have now been digitized, I find flipping through multiple electronic files and sites challenging when trying to compare a painting against period manuscripts. Additionally, there is a lot of duplication between books; some designs are in multiple books, and others in just one or two. I really wanted one reference source to look through, as well as to be able to study how the styles in embroidery designs changed over time, and when certain designs ceased to be popular.

To achieve this goal, I began by gathering and analyzing eight different 16th century German pattern books (Modelbücher) held at the Metropolitan Museum of Art, organizing the individual plates in each book by type (freestyle or charted), and stylistic elements.

To this compilation, I have added a section of historical artifacts which depict or use similar patterns to those found in these pattern books, which will inspire and guide you in your use of these patterns.

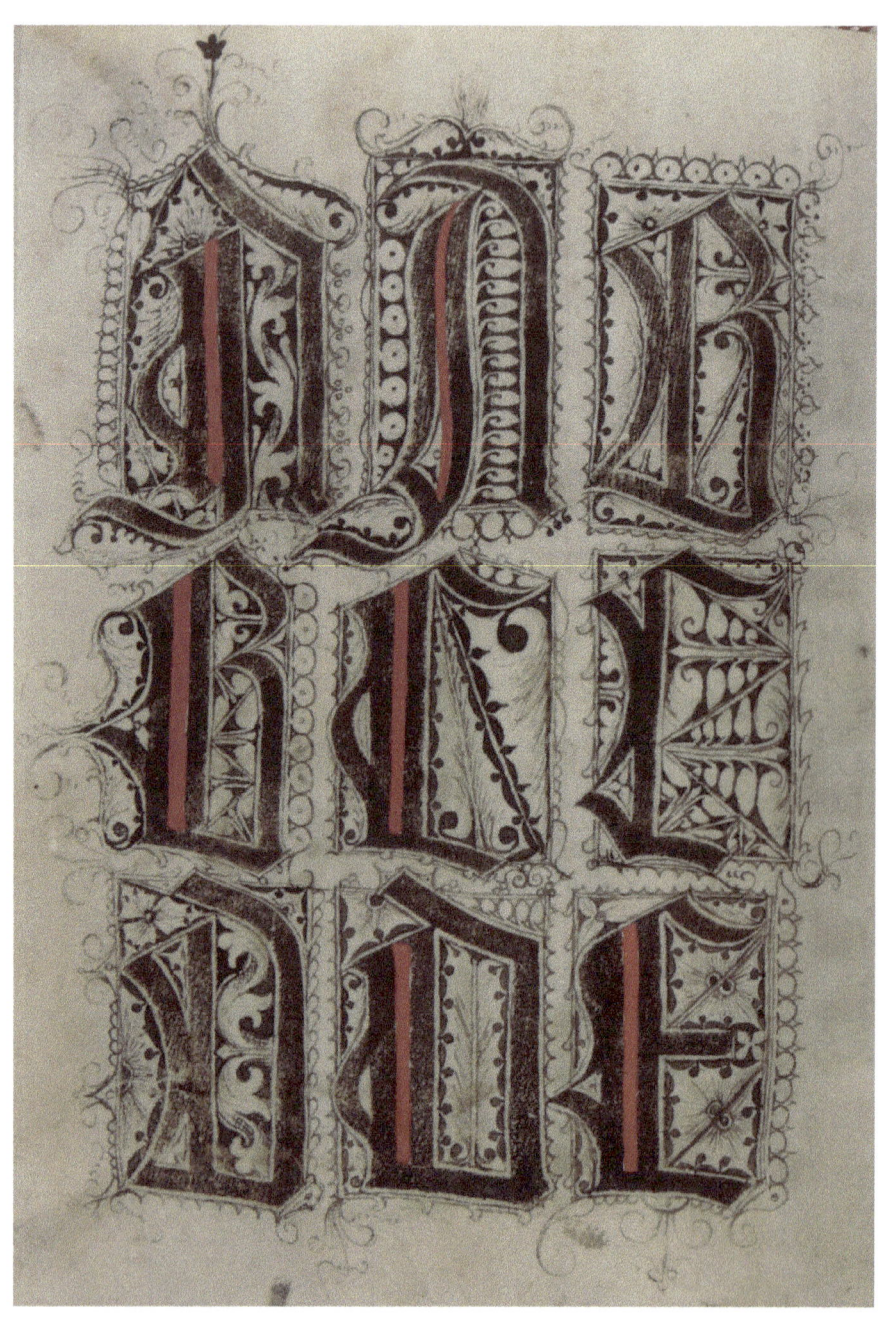

1. Letters A through E, from the Scribal pattern book, Gregorius Bock, ca. 1510 – 1517, f.28v
   Beinecke MS 439, Yale University Library

The Modelbücher

The word *Modelbuch* means "pattern book" or "model book" in German, and was first used by scribes to refer to the book of scribal samples they kept to show clients different styles (Fig. 1). Weavers also kept handwritten pattern books; the most famous surviving one is *Anna Neuper's Modelbuch*, in the Herzog August Bibliothek, which contains patterns for tabletwoven bands[1].

With the advent of the printing press, and the proliferation of woodcuts for book illustrations, it was only a matter of time before someone developed the idea of printing a book solely made of decorative designs. Johannes Schönsperger the Younger printed the earliest surviving example in Augsburg, Germany in 1523.[2] He printed another in 1524 in Zwickau, Germany, said to be "New and Improved" on the title page. This book proved to be such a bestseller, that he produced several others, including one in 1525 that it was quickly copied by Peter Quentel in Cologne in 1527. Quentel made a few slight modifications to the front page to change the headdress style of the weavers to match the local Cologne style and republished the designs under his own name with a few additions.
After Schönsperger went bankrupt,[3] Quentel would go on to republish many of his patterns, and others of his own as well, in many other editions, producing much clearer and better quality woodcut prints.
As time went on, other printers copied the patterns in Quentel's books, including Italian printers who copied his title page with the two ladies in Cologne-style dress weaving, and many of the designs[4], as well as adding their own too. Gülfferich's 1553 edition is a mix of material from Schönsperger, Quentel, and a few scattered original designs, which may have also been borrowed from other, yet unknown, pattern books.

Gülfferich was not the only one to have put together a collection of somewhat random plates into a book of patterns, Nicolas Bassée would do the same in his 1568 "New Modelbuch"[5] which republished Gülfferich's 1553 book, with some additional Italian designs. Whether he purchased the plates from Gülfferich or had new ones cut is unknown. Gülfferich does not appear to have used the same blocks as Schönsperger or Quentel, as a detailed examination of the woodcuts does not show the same printing flaws in the designs which are found in the different books.

Not everyone copied another book to produce their own. Hoffman's 1556 pattern book declares on the front page that his designs have never been put out in print, and indeed a comparison of the patterns in his book reveals only two plates of designs which are copied from another pattern book. The few plates that survive in Egenolff's 1535 pattern book are mostly unique, with a few borrowings from Quentel.

It is truly amazing that these books have survived at all, as they were working volumes, the pages torn out, used and destroyed as part of the creative process of weaving and needlework. Both Schönsperger's 1524 book and Egenolff's 1535 book are interesting examples of how thoroughly used these books were, with only portions of the original book surviving to the modern day.

Although Arthur Lotz published a very comprehensive bibliography in the 1930s[6], there is no complete list of all of the modelbücher which have ever been published. Attempts have been made to update Lotz's list with modern bibliographic search tools[7], but so much has been lost through heavy usage, wars, and the ravages of time, that some mysteries of where a pattern originally came from will never be known.

The Manuscripts

This book consists of the complied plates of the following eight pattern books located at the Metropolitan Museum of Art:

· Schönsperger's 1524 and 1529 editions
· Quentel's 1529, 1532, and 1544 editions
· Egenolff's 1535 edition
· Gülfferich's 1553 edition
· Hoffman's 1556 edition

Many designs are duplicated across various books, so they have been consolidated, with each plate appearing once, followed by a list of the book and folio number where it is located.

When other copies of the same or similar manuscript exist in another museum, Bibliothèque nationale de France (BnF Gallica), Staatliche Museen zu Berlin, or other institutions, they will be mentioned in the commentary on the book included here, but the plates of those manuscripts have not been included in the compilation of this book.

2.Hoffman 1556 f.28r, A lady with a box loom

Schönsperger 1524 f.1r

Schönsperger 1524

Ein new Modelbuch
Johann Schönsperger the Younger, Zwickau
Dimensions: 7 5/16 x 5 3/8 in. (18.5 x 13.6 cm)
Metropolitan Museum of Art, Gift of Herbert N. Straus, 1929
Accession Number: 29.71(1-31)

Ein New	A new pattern book for
Modelbüch auff außne-	needlework and borders,
he[n] vn[d] porten wircke[n] in d[er]	To be worked on the box frame
Laden vnd langen ge-	loom and the long weaving frame
stell Germert vn[d] ge-	New and improved, with new and
pessert mitt new.	different patterns.
andern Mö-	Published in the year 1524
deln.	
Anna d[omini] 1524.	
Eyn Model Büchleyn / Darauß	(on the back of the title page)
leycht-	A Model-booklet / From which
lich das Gewürck dyser nach	the working easily from these
angezeygten	displayed
Formen / erlernet warden mag. Be-	shapes / may be learned.
Druckt in der Fürstliche[n] Stadt	Printed in the Princely City
Zwickaw / durch Hanns	Zwickau / by Hanns
Schönsperger / Am xxii Octobris /	Schönsperger / on the 22nd of
Anno xxiiii	October
	Year 24

This book appears to be a rebound edition of at least two different copies of Schönsperger's Zwickau 1524 edition, including 10 duplicate pages, plus a few random pages of a similar style of pattern from Quentel's 1529 edition. Although the frontispiece mentions that charted patterns are included for use in weaving on the box loom and the larger weaving frame, it is missing this section.

There are editions dated slightly later, 1526 and 1527, of this same book held at the Bibliothèque nationale de France and the Staatliche Museen zu Berlin, which are not missing pages, and show that it was very similar in content to the 1529 edition.

Anno 1559 29

Ein new getruckt model Büchli auff auß nehen/ vnnd bortten wircken ynn der laden/ vnnd lanngenn gestell.

Ganntz gerecht nach abteilung der seden zal.

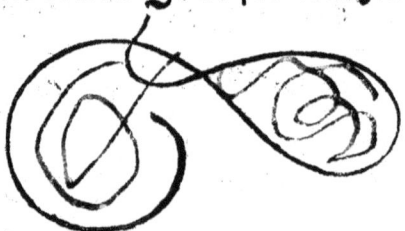

Schönsperger 1529

Ein new getruckt model Büchli
Johann Schönsperger the Younger, Augsburg
Dimensions: 7 ⅞ x 6 ⅛ in. (20 x 15.5 cm)
Metropolitan Museum of Art, Rogers Fund, 1918
Accession Number: 18.66.2(1-51)

1529	1529
Ein new getruckt	A new printed model book for
model Büchli auff aufnehen /	needlework
Und bortten wircken ynn der laden/	And borders worked in the box
Und lanngenn gestell	frame loom
Ganntz gerecht nach	And the long weaving frame
Abteilung der fedentzal	A whole section prepared for the
	counted thread designs

This copy of Schönsperger's 1529 edition is complete, and includes the collar band designs seen in the 1524 edition, the charted patterns (which were missing in the Metropolitan Museum's 1524 edition), and a new type of pattern, Spanish stitch, or what is now known as double running stitch. These Spanish stitch designs would be copied by other German pattern books, without many changes or additions.
In the blank pages at the end of the book, someone has transcribed several of the charted patterns into a weaving notation for ease of use.

Quentel 1529 f.1r

Quentel 1529

Eyn new kunstlichboich
Peter Quentel, woodcuts by Anton Woensam von Worms, Cologne
Dimensions: 7 ⅞ x 5 ½ in. (20 x 14 cm)
Metropolitan Museum of Art, Rogers Fund, 1920
Accession Number: 20.50.2(1-49)

Eyn new kunstlich boich / dairyn.C.und. Xxxviii , fi: guren /mostner ad[er] stalen befonden /
wie man na der rechter art / Lauffer werk / Spanische stiche / mit der nä: len / vort vp der Ramen / und vp der laden / borden wirchenn sal / wilche stalen alltzo samen verbessert synt/ und vyl kunstlicher gemacht / da[n] dye eirsten. Etc. Sere nutzlich allen wapen Sticker/frauwen, ionfferen/ und met ger/dair uß solch kunst lichtlich tzu
leren.

Gedrucht zu Cöllen vp dem Doemhoff durch Peter quentell Anno. M. D. XXIX

A new artful book containing located therein C XXXVIII (138) figures / patterns or styles / how one in the right way / running work / Spanish stitch / with the needle / for on the frame / and on the loom / borders should work / Which designs were altogether improved / and
made more craftily / than the first etc. Very useful for all coat of arms embroiderers / women, maidens / and carvers / to easily learn this art

Printed at Köln on the Domhoff (Cathedral Courtyard) by Peter Quentell Anno 1529

Quentel began publishing this edition in 1527, and was very successful with it, continuing to publish the same book until 1535. This book, published in 1529, was aimed at the export market as it contains an Italian translation of the title page. The designs come from various sources; the charted and Spanish stitch designs were mainly copied from Schönsperger's 1526 edition of "Ein new modelbuch", with a few additions from Schönsperger's 1527 – 1529 "F(urm oder modelbüchlein".[8] Quentel did not copy Schönsperger's collar designs, replacing them instead with new designs of his own.

German Modelbücher 1524 – 1556

Quentel 1532 f.1r

Quentel 1532

Eyn Newe kunstlich moetdelboech alle kunst
Peter Quentel, Cologne
Dimensions: Overall: 5 $^{11}/_{16}$ x 8 $^{1}/_{16}$ in. (14.5 x 20.5 cm)
Metropolitan Museum of Art, Harris Brisbane Dick Fund, 1924
Accession Number: 24.29(1-32)

Eyn newe kunstlich moetdelboech alle kunstner
zo brauchen fur snytzeller / wapensticker perlensticker etc. vnd ouch fur Jonferen vnd frauwen / ernstlich vff das neuwes gefonde[n] alle[n] den gene[n] vff kunste[n] verstant habent.
Gedruckt zo Collen, durch Peter Quentel. Jiniar, M..D.XXXII. im Bramaent.

A new artful modelbuch [that] all artists might need for cutters / heraldic embroiderer pearl embroiderer etc. and also for maidens and wives / earnestly newly found for those who understand the arts.

Printed in Colgne, by Peter Quentel. June 1532, in June (Brachmonat)

Quentel's "New artful pattern book" of 1532 contains many new freestyle designs for different uses, and just a few charted patterns copied from Schönsperger's 1527 – 1529 "F(urm oder modelbüchlein". The illustration on the title page depicts a woodcarver at the top, and three ladies in a row on the bottom: on the left, embroidering on a frame; center, stitching or embroidering without a frame; right, weaving on a box loom. The designs in the book are full of flourishes, swirls, and putti, perhaps influenced by Italian pattern books which had been imported.

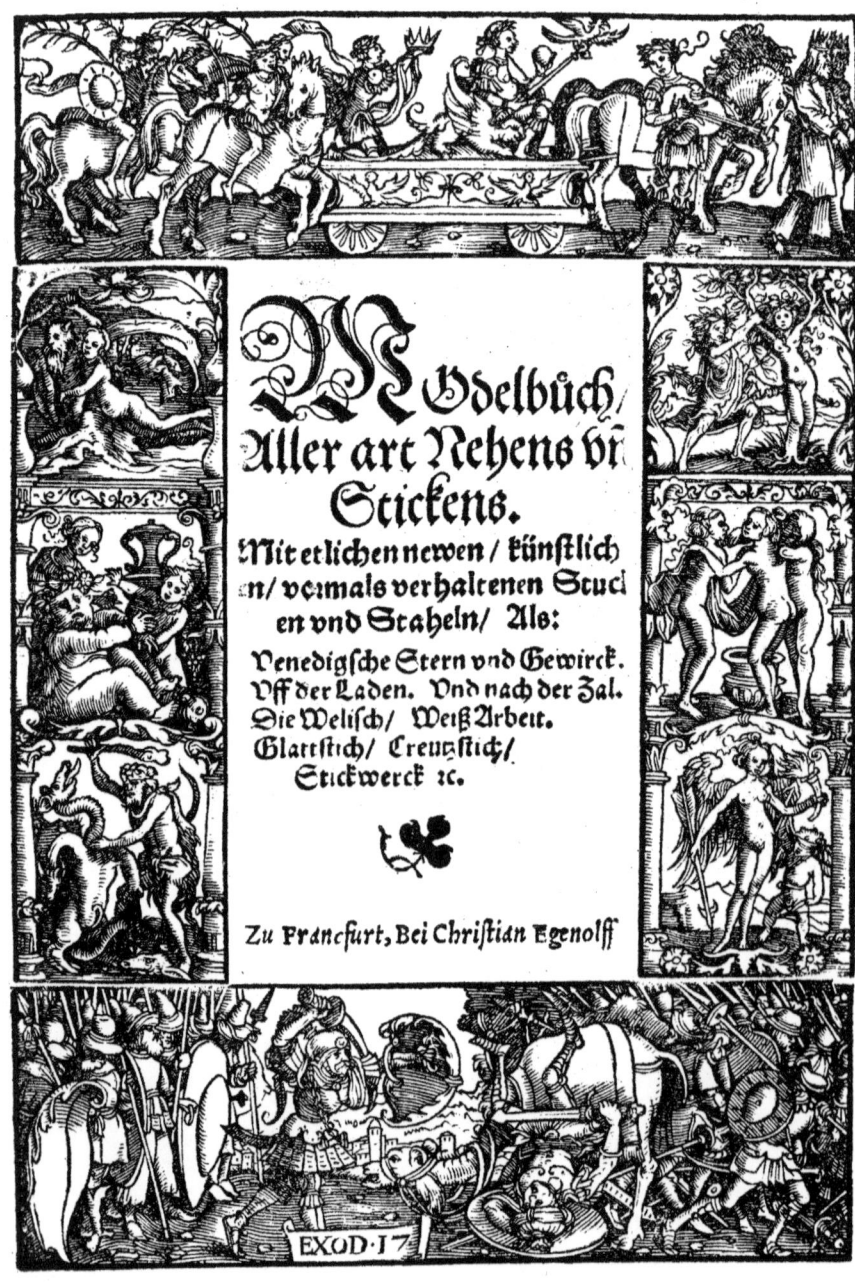

Egenolff 1535 f.1r

Introduction

Egenolff 1535

Modelbuch aller Art Nehens vn Stickens
Christian Egenolff, Frankfurt am Main
Dimensions: 7 5/16 x 5 5/16 in. (18.5 x 13.5 cm)
Metropolitan Museum of Art, Harris Brisbane Dick Fund, 1933
Accession Number: 33.69(1-27)

Modelbuch	A pattern book / of all kinds
Aller art Nehens vn[d] Stickens	Sewing and embroidery, with
Mit etlichen newen kunstlich[-]en	some new / artful / formerly held
vormals verhaltenen Stuck/ en und	pieces and styles / such as
Staheln/ Als:/	Venetian Stars and the like,
Venedigsche Stern und Gerwirck	Work on the frame [box loom]?
Uff der Laden. Und nach der Zal.	and by the count
Die Welisch/ Weiss Arbeit./	the Italian / white work
Glattstich/ Creustick/ Stickwerck zc.	Flat stitch / Cross stitch /
	embroidery etc.
/Zu Frankfurt, Bei Christian Egenolff	At Frankfurt, by Christian Egenolff

Egenolff's 1535 book is an interesting example of how thoroughly used these books were, with only portions of this original book surviving to the modern day. The few plates that survive are mostly unique, with a few obvious borrowings from Quentel. An examination of a later, but similar, 1555 edition of his book held at the Bayerische Staatsbibliothek[9] reveals that many of his designs in the book were copied and redrawn from Italian pattern books.

Ⓔn new kunſtlich Model=
buch/ dair yn meir dan Sechßhundert
figuren/monſter ader ſtalen beſondenn/
wie mann na der rechter art/ Perlenſtic=
kers/Lauffer werck/ Spanſche ſtiche/
mit der nalen/vort vp der Ramen/vnd
vp der laden/borden wircken ſal/ wilche
ſtalen al tzo ſamen verbeſſert ſint/ vñ vil kunſtlicher gemacht/
dan die eirſten mit vil meir neuwe ſtalen hier by geſatz ꝛc.
Sere nutzlich alle/wapenſticker/ frauwen/ionfferen/vnd met=
ger/ dair vß ſolch kunſt lichtlich tzo lerenn

Vng Nouiau liure auerpluſeurs ſciences et patrons qui
nont point eſtes encoꝛ impꝛimes.

¶Gedruckt tzo Cöllen vp dem Doemhoff
durch Peter Quentell.

Im jair   M. D. XLIIII.

Quentel 1544 f.1r

Quentel 1544

Ein new kunstlich Modelbuch ...
Peter Quentel, Cologne
Dimensions: 7 11/16 x 5 7/8 in. (19.5 x 15 cm)
Metropolitan Museum of Art, Rogers Fund, 1922
Accession Number: 22.84.1(1-102)

EIn new kunstlich Model:
Büch dairy n meir dan Sechßhundert
Figuren / monster ader stalen
befondenn / Wie mann na der
rechter art / Perlenstic:kers / Lauffer
wreck / Spansche stiche / mit der
nälen / vort vp der Ramen / vnd
vp der laden / border wircken sal /
wilche Stalen altzosamen verbessert
sint / vn[d] viel kunstlicher gemacht
/ Dan die ersten mit vil meir
neuwe stalen hier by gesatz etc.
Sere nutzlich alle / wapensticker /
frauwen / ionfferen / vnd met:ger
/ dair vß solch kunst lichtlich tzo
lerenn

Ung Nouviau livre avec pluseurs
sciences et patrons qui nont poinct
estes encore imprimes

Gedruckt tzo Cöllen vp dem
Doemhoff
Durch Peter Quentell
Im jair MD XLIIII

A new artful book containing
located therein C XXXVIII (138)
figures / patterns or styles / how
one in the right way / running
work / Spanish stitch / with the
needle / for on the frame / and
on the loom / borders should
work / Which designs were
altogether improved / and made
more craftily / than the first etc.
Very useful for all coat of arms
embroiderers / women, maidens
/ and carvers / to easily learn this
art

(From French):
A new book with many
knowledges and patterns that
never have been before printed.

Printed in Köln on the Domhoff
(Cathedral courtyard)
By Peter Quentell
In the year 1544.

Quentel's "New artful pattern book" of 1544 contains most of the patterns in his 1529 and 1532
editions, plus additional new freestyle and charted patterns. The title page is a simplified
version of his 1532 title page, to allow for his extensive description of the types of patterns,
methods they can be worked, and who would benefit from the book. The book appears to be
complete, and is similar in content to two earlier editions, 1536 in the Bayerische
Staatsbibliothek, and 1541 in Bibliotheque nationale de France.

Modelbuch New/

aller art/ Nehens vnd Stickens.
Jetzundt wider mit viel schönen Mo-
delen vnnd Stahlen / Allen Steinmetzen/
Schreinern/Seidenstickern/vnd Ne-
derinnen / sehr Nützlich vnd lu-
stig zugericht.

Gedruckt zu Franckfurdt am Mayn/
durch Herman Gülfferichen.

M. D. LIII.

Introduction

Gülfferich 1553

Modelbuch new, aller Art, Nehens und Stickens
Hermann Gülfferich, Frankfurt am Main
Dimensions: 6 ⅞ x 4 ¹⁵⁄₁₆ in. (17.5 x 12.5 cm)
Metropolitan Museum of Art, Harris Brisbane Dick Fund, 1923
Accession Number: 23.40(1-78)

Modelbuch New/
aller art/ Nehens und Stickens.
Jetzundt wider mit viel schönen Mö:
delen vnnd Stahlen / Allen
Steinmetzen/
Schreinern / Seidenstickern / und Ne:
derinnen / sehr Nützlich und lü:
stig zugericht.

Gedruckt zu Franckfurdt am Mayn /
Durch Herman Gülfferichen.
M. D. LIII

Modelbuch New /
all sorts of / sewing and
embroidery.
Now and again with many pretty
patterns
and styles / all stone cutters /
carpenters / silk embroiderers /
and seamstresses / very usefully
and enjoyably presented.

Printed in Frankfurt am Main /
By Herman Gülfferichen.
1553

Gülfferich's 1553 edition is a mix of material from Quentel's 1544 edition and a few original designs for satin stitch, "glattstitch", which may have also been borrowed from other, yet unknown, pattern books. The charted patterns were printed very badly, perhaps due to old blocks being used for the printing.

New Modelbůch/

Allen Nägerin/ vnnd Sydenstickern

Sehr nutzlich zů brauchē/vor nye in Druck außgangen/
durch Hans Hoffman/ Burger vnd Form-
schneider zů Straßburg.

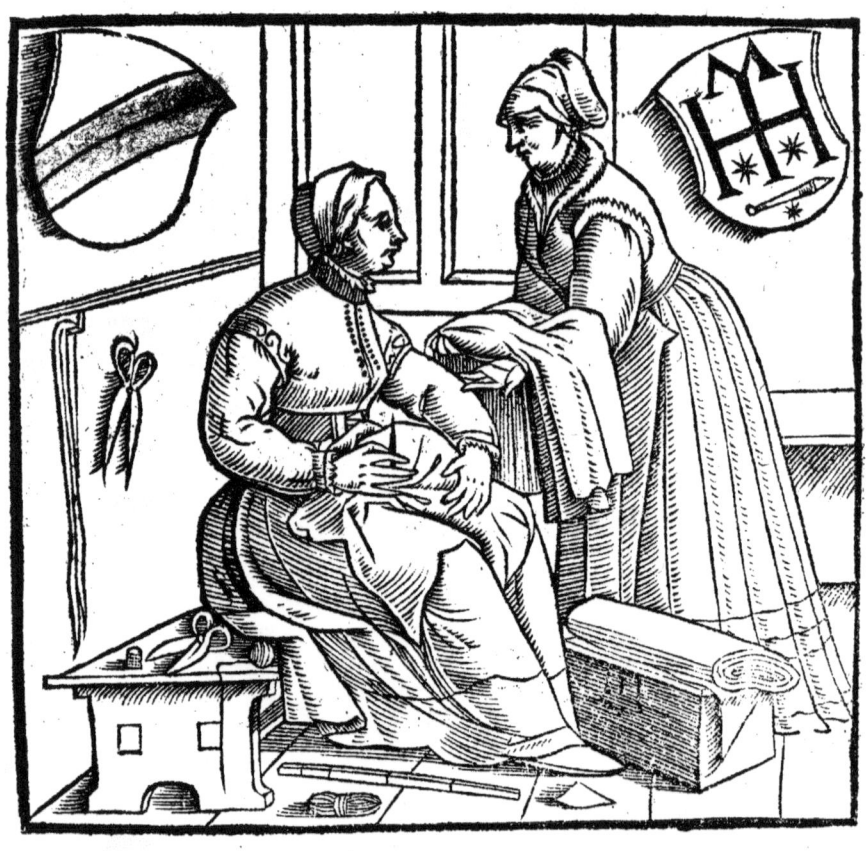

Hoffman 1556 f.1r

Introduction

Hoffman 1556

New Modelbuch allen Nägerin u. Sydenstickern
Hans Hoffman, Strasbourg
Dimensions: 7 5/16 x 5 5/16 in. (18.5 x 13.5 cm)
Metropolitan Museum of Art, Harris Brisbane Dick Fund, 1930
Accession Number: 30.59.2(1-55)

New Modelbuch /	New Modelbuch
Allen Nägerin / vnnd Sydenstickern	For all seamstresses / and silk embroiderers
Sehr nutzlich zü brauche[n]/	Very useful for [their] needs/
Vor nye in Druck außgangen/	Never before put out in print/
Durch Hans Hoffman / Borger vnd Form-	By Hans Hoffman / Citizen and Woodcutter of Strassburg
Schneider zü Straßburg	

Not everyone copied another book to produce their own. Hoffman's pattern book declares on the front page that his designs have never been put out in print, and indeed a comparison of the patterns in his book reveals only two plates of designs are copied from another pattern book. The title page depicts a seamstress at work, with a customer who has brought more work for her. Other illustrations in the book depict a lady at a tapestry loom, p. 56, and another at a box loom, p. 9.
The designs in the book are a mix of ornate filigree designs for cord work and embroidery, and fanciful freestyle designs which could be used for many different types of work.

Introduction

Woven Bands and Fabric

It is not surprising that Peter Quentel, located in Cologne, would choose to publish his own edition of Schönsperger's pattern book. The charted band patterns are very similar to those seen on the woven gold belts, and headdress bands depicted in portraits from the Cologne area (Fig. 10). From the 12th to the 16th century, Cologne was famous for its woven golden bands, *Kölner borte,* used both for church garments (Fig. 5) and as a part of upper class womens fashion.[10] In other areas of Germany, the wide woven gold bands were also used as *brustfleck,* a decorative band, used to fill in the neckline of women's gowns (Fig. 12)

Both Schönsperger and Quentel depict two different types of looms, *langen gestell,* a large weaving frame (Fig. 3), and *laden,* a small box loom (Fig. 4). Schönsperger's depiction of the *langen gestell* is a simplified drawing of the loom unfortunately, but it does show cords on the right, passing through a round plate which could be draw cords for a draw loom. Although the lady is using a simple rigid heddle, there are foot pedals, indicating that there was most likely a more complex heddle arrangement than the artist wished to depict.

The complex twill weave of the Cologne-style bands would have required the use of a draw loom, whereas the smaller box loom, *laden,* would have been used for less complicated bands.
While the *langen gestell* appears to have fallen out of use for weaving, the *laden* is mentioned or depicted by all of the pattern books, except Gülfferich.

3. A lady weaving on a long weaving frame, langen gestell Schönsperger 1524, f.1r

4. A lady weaving on a box loom, laden, detail from Quentel 1532, f.1r

German Modelbücher 1524 – 1556

5. Front and back of a Cologne Band, with the text Jesus Maria on a golden ground between flowers and tree. 1425 – 1449 Linen, silk, gold thread. Weft-faced compound twill. Museum Catharijneconvent, Utrecht, photo by Ruben de Heer, Inv.: ABM t2285b

Introduction

This lovely example of a 15th c. Cologne band, *Kölner borte*, can be seen from both the front and back sides. Ecclesiastical bands such as this were woven using a weft-faced compound twill, with a linen warp, primary weft of gold thread, and a secondary weft linen or silk[11]. This band would have been woven on a draw loom, likely a *langen gestell*. Many examples of *Kölner borte* survive in museum collections, woven in similar manner and style.

The tree and flowering bush with red and white flowers were common motifs, as was an eight-petaled flower (Fig.6 and 9). Schönsperger and Quentel both included upper and lower case alphabets and similar styled flowers and trees in their pattern books. In his 1544 edition, Quentel included a full page of different religious motifs commonly seen in these bands (plate 194).

6. Detail of 15th c woven Cologne band, silk, linen and gold thread.
Metropolitan Museum of Art, Rogers Fund, 1909, Accession Number: 09.50.976

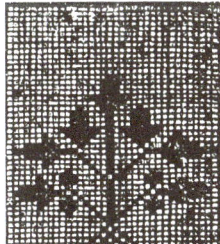 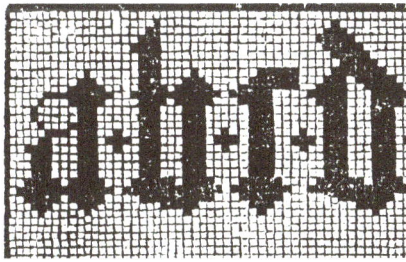 

7. (left) Detail from plate 194
8. (middle) Detail from plate 188, lower case a, b, c, d
9. (right) Detail from plate 189

German Modelbücher 1524 – 1556

10. *Portrait of Elisabeth Bellinghausen, Bartholomäus Bruyn (l), 1538 – 1539 Rijksmuseum, Amsterdam SK-A-2559, (below) Detail of belt*

Introduction

In her portrait, Elizabeth Bellinghausen wears the upper class fashionable style dress from Cologne, with a beautiful woven gold belt, deep gold band over her bust, narrow gold bands on her parlet, and another woven gold band at her forehead. The headband is very thin and flexible as it easily forms to the curve of her head. The band on the belt is sewn to a thick red fabric for stability. The pattern of the headband is a diamond pattern with stars, similar to plate 150. The belt is similar to several patterns, but not identical, with elements of several of the bands being combined from plates 139 and 141.

A similar type of gold woven band is found on the edge of a 15th century *palla*, a ceremonial cover used in the Catholic Mass. The woven gold band has a metallic thread weft and a silk floss warp. A side view of the *palla* allows for a close-up of the band's structure, revealing a loosely woven patterned float weave, which allows for the silk to shimmer behind the metal, increasing the glimmer of the band.

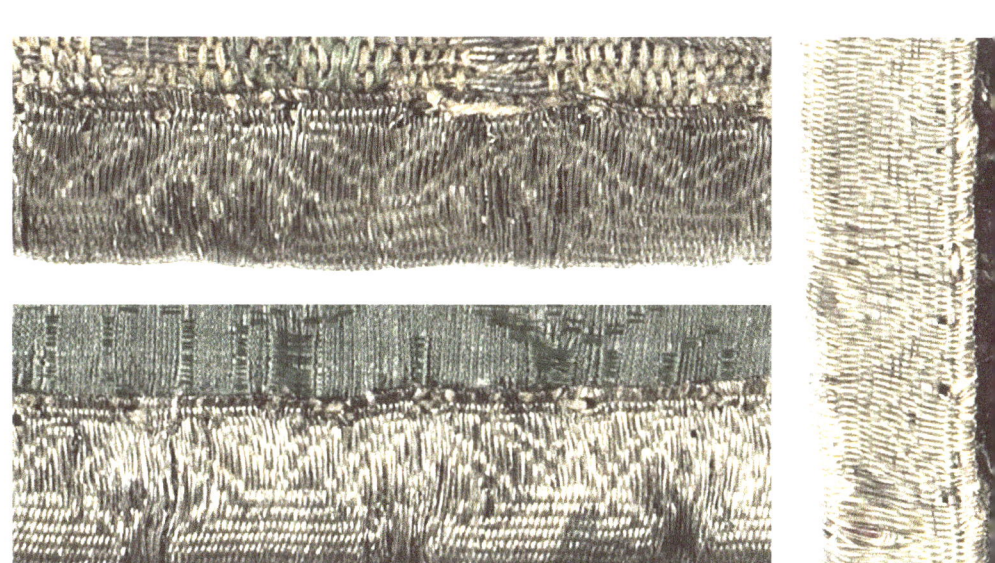

11. Detail of metal border front, back, and side from red palla with crucifixion, edged with metal border, back of green silk. Lower Rhine, between 1475 and 1499. Museum Catharijneconvent, Utrecht, photo Ruben de Heer, Inv.No.: RMCC t40

German Modelbücher 1524 – 1556

12. Margarethe Vöhlin, Wife of Hans Roth [obverse], 1527 Bernhard Strigel, National Gallery of Art, Washington D.C., Ralph and Mary Booth Collection 1947. 6.5.a (lower left) Detail of brustfleck
13. Similar pattern from plate 179.

Introduction

Cologne wasn't the only place to feature woven gold bands as part of upper class fashion. This lovely portrait of Margarethe Vöhlin (Fig. 12) shows a deep woven gold *brustfleck*, filling in the low neckline of her dress. A close-up of the piece shows that the painter depicted the gold as both warp and weft, with long floats. The diamond pattern is similar to the middle band of plate 179.

The *brustfleck* may have been woven using a supplemental warp and weft, with a primary linen or silk warp, as seen on the band in Fig. 14. An undamaged section, left, reveals how the band originally looked, with the color of the primary warp showing through the metal, illuminating the design. The damaged section on the right, allows a clear view of the woven structure. The design is similar to the upper band of plate 148, with an edging of diamonds, found at the bottom of plate 140.

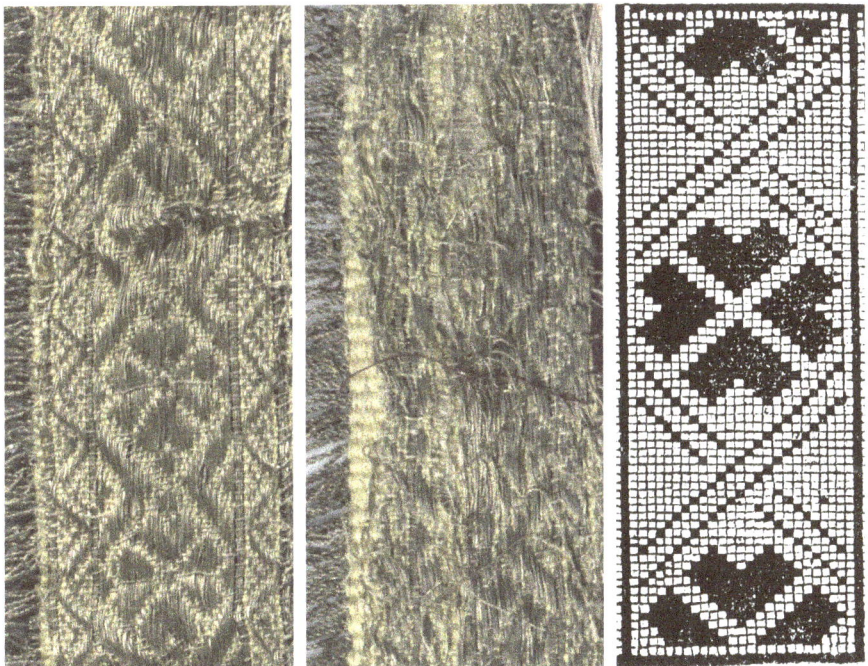

14. Detail of gold edging, undamaged and damaged section from a tablecloth of silk velvet, finished with gold edging and gold fringe, 1600 – 1699, Rijksmuseum, Amsterdam BK-17295
15. Similar pattern from plate 139.

Another method of weaving a gold band is shown here, in this tightly woven float patterned band from a 15th century dalmatic. It is woven with a thin red silk warp and a weft of gold thread. The band is identical on both sides, with the front being embroidered with couching and embroidered slips (not shown). The pattern of interlaced strips is similar to the upper band on plate 177.

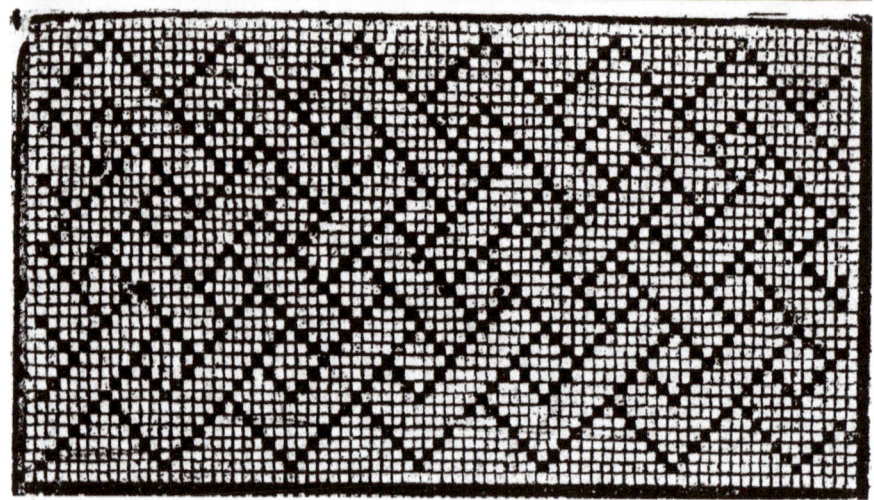

16. *Fragment of a band from a dalmatic, silk warp and gold thread weft. Germany (possibly), c. 1475 – 1500, Rijksmuseum Amsterdam BK-NM-4165-D-3*
17. *Detail from plate 177*

Introduction

Gold was of course not the only material woven into patterns. This 16th–17th century linen damask napkin was woven in a variation of the pattern on plate 183. The weaver rotated the design 45 degrees, changing the motif of the pattern in Fig.20 from interlinked diamonds to squares.

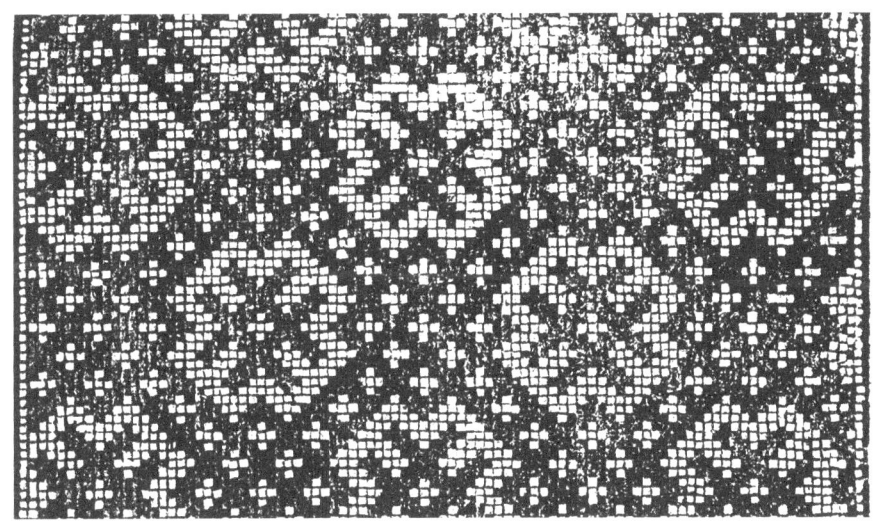

18. (left) Linen damask napkin, 1600 – 1650, Rijksmuseum Amsterdam. BK-1977-323-A
19. (right) Rotated 45 degrees to match pattern
20. Pattern from plate 183

Weavers often changed or modified patterns to suit the project. In this section of a 16th century Italian linen woven sampler, the weaver chose to change the diagonal lines to intersect in the middle of the flowers, instead of the squares, as is seen on the original pattern on plate 153. The fabric is woven with a white linen tabby ground, and supplemental blue linen weft.

21. *Piece of a blue and white linen woven sampler, Italian, 16th c.*
    Metropolitan Museum of Art, Gift of Marian Hague, 1938, Accession Number: 38.185.22
22. *Pattern from plate 153*

Introduction

In this 16th century Italian or German linen band, the weaver combined a eight-petaled flower pattern, seen in Fig. 22, with a shortened section of the diamond and bar pattern in Fig. 24 to create a new design. The band is woven with a blue linen tabby woven ground and white linen supplemental warp.

23. Band, Italian or German, 16th c.
    Metropolitan Museum of Art, Gift of Marian Hague, 1938, Accession Number: 38.185.2
24. Detail from plate 145.

Embroidery and Needlework

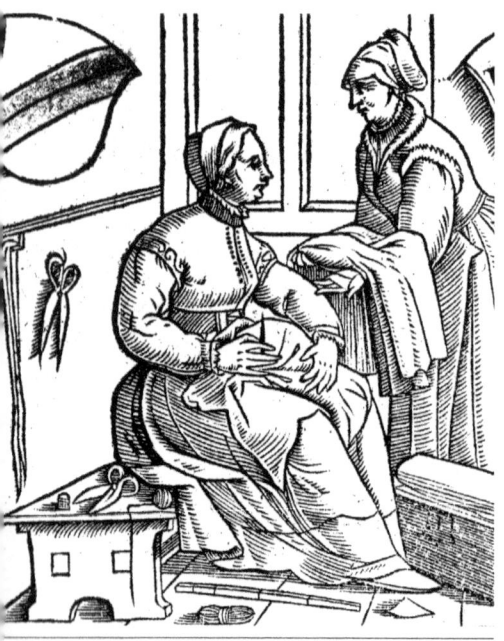

25. Seamstress at work, detail from Hoffman 1556 f.1r

The seamstress sits at her bench, surrounded by her tools, needle in her hand (Fig. 25). Scissors hang on a hook on the wall behind her, next to a strip of parchment or paper for measuring. Her thimble, scissors, and a ball of thread are on the bench beside her, an ell measuring stick and more thread on the floor. A customer has come in, carrying fabric, perhaps to commission a new shirt for a husband, son, or herself. The seamstress pauses her work to speak to the customer... Perhaps she pulls out a sampler book (Fig. 55) to discuss embroidery designs for the collar and cuffs.

While ecclesiastical embroideries are the most frequent survivors in museum collections today, the majority of embroidery in the 16th century would have been for shirts and other body linens. However, since very few of these linen garments have survived, the only record we have of their existence is in paintings and other artwork.

In the early to middle 16th century, the most common style of shirt seen on men in artwork had a very full pleated body, with the fullness handled in different ways at the neck. On some shirts, Fig. 27 and 29, the body is pleated, and the pleats secured with threads, creating the collar, which is then darned with a pattern. Other shirts have a separate gold worked collar, Fig. 31, and the linen collar of the shirt is obscured and not visible. Towards the middle of the 16th century, a different style of shirt collar came into fashion, Fig. 43 and 49,(a band that the shirt was gathered into, with a separate ruffle). Women wore a variety of shirts, smocks, and gollars (partlets), with the collars handled in a variety of ways, including pattern darned collars.

Pleated Shirts

In the Museum of London's collection, there are two 16th century fine woolen sleeve fragments[12] which are tightly pleated, and decorated with a darned pattern, as is seen on the collars of Fig. 27 and 29. The wool has been pleated and secured with gathering threads, but the pleats are not secured with smocking stitches. Silk floss has been used to create a pattern on the pleats, by weaving the silk above and below the surface of the pleats as if the pleats are the warp and the silk thread is the weft in a piece of weaving. This appears to be what the two young women are working on in Fig. 26. One is at a frame, pleating a piece of fabric, and the other has a pleated panel in her lap, stitching the design on the collar, a pattern book is open on the table next to them.

Diamond patterns were very popular for collars, judging by the styles depicted in paintings and sculptures. The shirt in Fig. 27 is darned with a closely-packed diamond-within-diamond pattern, the tiny pleats creating a small ruffle at the top of the collar, while the shirt in Fig. 29 is darned with a larger, more open pattern, and appears to have some surface embroidery along with the pattern. The pleats are secured further from the top edge, allowing for a longer ruffle at the top.

26. Detail of two young women sewing shirts from the title page from Paganini's "Il Burato: libro de recami" which he copied from Schönsperger's 1523 pattern book[13]

German Modelbücher 1524 – 1556

27. Portrait of Cornelis Aerentsz van der Dussen, copy after Jan van Scorel c.1555 – c.1570 Rijksmuseum, Amsterdam SK-A-1532 (lower left) Detail of collar
28. Lower band of plate 151

29. Hans Roth, 1527, Bernhard Strigel, National Gallery of Art, Washington D.C., Ralph and Mary Booth Collection, 1947.6.4.a (lower left) Detail of white work collar and buttons
30. Lower band from plate 176

German Modelbücher 1524 – 1556

31. Posthumous Portrait of Rudolph van Buynou (d 1542), High Bailiff of Stavoren and 'Grietman' of Gaasterland, Adriaen van Cronenburg, 1553 Rijismuseum, Amsterdam SK-A-1993 (middle) Detail of gold work collar
32. Similar pattern, from plate 54

Introduction

Goldwork and Pearls

Not all pleated shirts had a pattern darned collar, some had a separate embroidered neckband (Fig. 31). This neckband is worked in a diamond pattern, similar to plate 54 (Fig. 32), with gold thread and pearls.

It was probably worked in a similar fashion as this trim from a 1520s chausible (Fig. 33). Here, the gold thread is laid down and caught with red silk. The gold thread is padded underneath to highlight the pattern and catch the light. This padded goldwork band is worked in a similar zig-zag pattern as the top band in plate 142 (Fig. 34).

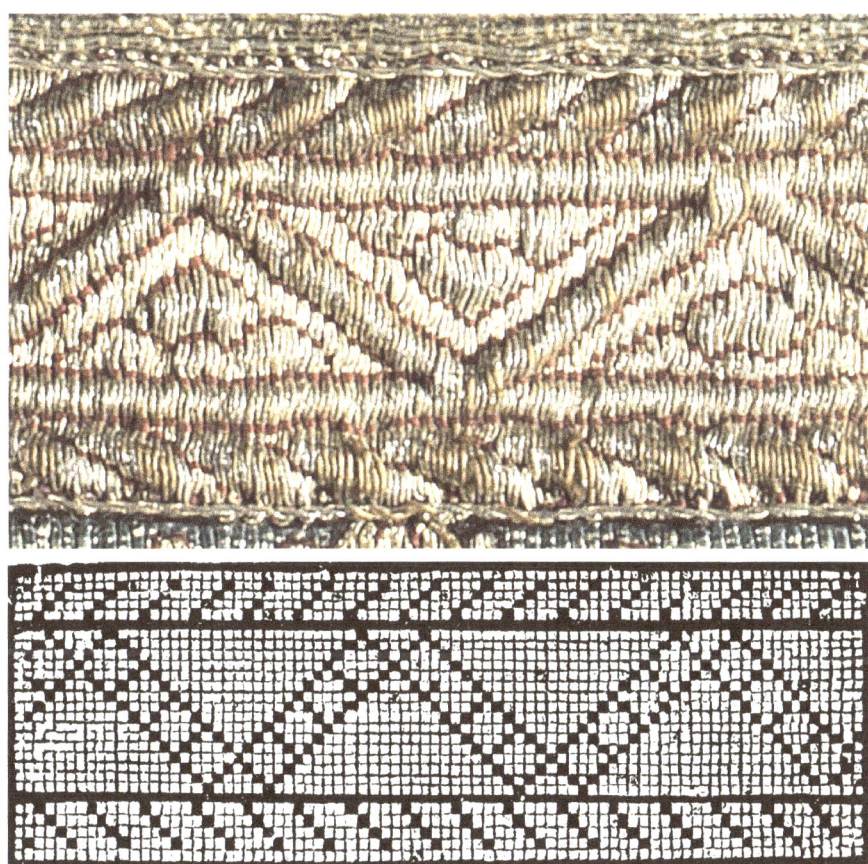

33. Detail from red chasuble with scenes from the life of Simon and Judas Thaddeus and the bread multiplication, Museum Catharijneconvent, Utrecht, photo Ruben de Heer Inventory number: BMH t5788a
34. Top band from plate 142

43

German Modelbücher 1524 – 1556

35. Pouch of purple velvet, embroidered with multicolored silk, gold thread, pearls, beads and rubies 1600 – 1625, Rijksmuseum, Amsterdam BK-NM-11110
36. Band from plate 103

Introduction

This lovely embroidered bag was most likely the work of a professional embroider, probably commissioned to celebrate a marriage, their initials of DG and ML are worked into the bag's design. The curving gold cords, interlaced, and sprouting flowers, with the center point a pair of clasped hands are similar, but not identical, to patterns seen in Hoffman's 1556 book. Professional embroiders were expected to develop their own designs, but the maker of this piece may have used Hoffman's book as inspiration, or as a tool in the consultation with the customer to determine the desired type of design.

The velvet was originally purple, but has faded with time. A gold cord made of twisted passing threads is couched almost invisibly with matching gold-colored silk floss, and highlights the flowers and leaves made of freshwater pearls and now tarnished silver purl. Silver purl beads wrap around freshwater pearls and adorn the ground between elements along with short sections of silver lizardine. The clasped hands at the center are stitched with silk floss, with cuffs worked in silver thread.

Satin Stitch with Gold Work

The cuff of this elaborate Italian smock is worked in freestyle satin stitch and couched metallic thread. The gold thread appears to have been put down first, following the inked design, and then the red and blue silk stitched to fill in the open areas. A thin blue line of double running stitch is at the bottom edge of the cuff. The design is very similar to one from Hoffman's 1556 book (Fig. 38).

37. *Cuff of Smock, late 16th century Italian, linen, silk, and metal thread*
   Metropolitan Museum of Art, Rogers Fund, 1910, Accession Number: 10.124.1
38. *Top band from plate 101*

Introduction

Cord Work

Emilia di Spilimbergo, painted by Titian, wears a ropa decorated with passementerie, cord couched into interlaced designs. The pattern is similar to one found in Hoffman's book (Fig. 40). He published many designs for two, three, four or more cords. This design is a simple one of just two cords, which loop and knot around each other.

39. Emilia di Spilimbergo, c. 1560 , Follower of Titian,
    Widener Collection National Gallery of Art, Washington D.C. 1942.9.82
40. Bottom design from plate 91

Glattstich – Satin Stitch

Egenolff in his introduction, lists *glattstich* or flat stitch as one of the many stitches his patterns could be used for. Known today as satin stitch, this versatile stitch can be worked either as a counted or freestyle stitch.

This piece is a wonderful example of counted satin stitch and faggot stitch, worked in silk floss on linen (Fig. 41). The stars are crisply worked over one stitch per warp and weft thread. The diagonal checks are worked in faggot stitch over three threads. This shirt (Fig. 43) has a thin collar, unlike the thick collars of the pleated shirts. The collar has a diamond pattern with flowers, similar to Fig. 44, which gleams like silk floss on linen. It was most likely worked in satin stitch, along with other stitches.

41. Band, Satin and double running stitch, silk on linen, 16th century probably Spanish
    Metropolitan Museum of Art, Gift of Marian Hague, 1938, Accession Number: 38.185.19
42. Top band from plate 150

Introduction

43. *A Member of the de Hondecoeter Family, 1543, Probably Antwerp, 16th Century, National Gallery of Art, Washington D.C., Gift of Adolph Caspar Miller 1953.3.3.a (middle) Detail of white work collar*
44. *Top band from plate 145*

Weiss Arbeit – White Work

Weiss Arbeit, white work, is a general term for embroidery worked with white thread on white fabric, usually linen thread on linen fabric. Only Egenholf mentions that his pattern book contains patterns for *weiss arbeit*, but Gülfferich's pattern book contains pages of satin stitch designs, which is similar to Fig. 45. In 16th century embroidery, white work often incorporated, but was not limited to: areas of cutwork, open, pulled and drawn thread work, eyelets, needlelace, satin, and stem stitches.

45. Band with cutwork, drawnwork, bobbin lace and satin stitch, 16th – 17th century, German or Italian, Metropolitan Museum of Art, Rogers Fund, 1909, Accession Number: 09.50.3194
46. Designs for white work with satin stitch, Detail from plate 95

Introduction

Fig. 45 is an illustrative example of an elaborate white work piece. It is embroidered with silk floss on linen fabric, and is worked in counted satin stitch, pulled thread work, and cutwork with needlelace insertions.

However, most pieces were worked in linen thread on linen fabric, designed to decorate shirt collars, cuffs, and other linen garments which were needed to be washed. Fig. 47 is worked in linen thread on linen fabric, in satin stitch, drawn thread work, needle lace, and cutwork. Fig. 43 is an excellent example of white work without areas of cut or drawn thread work.

47. White work sample, done in cutwork, drawn thread work and satin stitch. 16th century Italian, Metropolitan Museum of Art, Rogers Fund, 1908, Accession Number: 08.194.7
48. Pattern with a similar four hearts motif from plate 139.
    Diamond pattern is similar to plate 179

German Modelbücher 1524 – 1556

49. Portrait of Anna of Lorraine, possibly copy after Jan van Scorel, after 1542
    Rijksmuseum, Amsterdam SK-A-4027
50. Band from plate 28

Introduction

Spanish Stitch – Double Running, and Cross Stitch

Another common decoration stitch for shirt collars and cuffs was Spanish stitch, or double running stitch, with the design appearing the same on both sides, thus allowing the collar to be worn open or closed. In Fig. 49, the collar is worked in Spanish stitch, the pattern showing inside and outside. The interlaced pattern is similar to one found in Egenholff's pattern book (Fig.50).

A simpler interlaced pattern was stitched in an early 17th Portuguese sampler book. The green silk is stitched over two threads in double running stitch (Fig. 51). It is similar to a pattern found in Quentel's 1544 book (Fig. 52).

Double running and long-armed cross stitch designs are closely related in the pattern books, often being shown as the reverse of each other (Fig. 54). Here the embroider has done one floral motif, and then filled one half in long-armed cross stitch, creating a section of Assisi stitch (Fig. 53). This floral pattern is not found in any of the German pattern books, and is most likely an Italian design.

51. Detail of spiral pattern, worked in green silk from Booklet of embroidery and drawnwork, early 17th century, probably Portuguese, Metropolitan Museum of Art, Gift of Miss Mary Parsons, 1925, Accession Number: 25.92

52. Pattern from plate 137

53. Detail of floral chain pattern, worked in red silk, from Booklet of Embroidery and Drawnwork, Metropolitan Museum of Art, Gift of Miss Mary Parsons, 1925, Accession Number: 25.92
54. Pattern from plate 133

Embroiderers may have used a sampler pattern book, as in Fig. 55, to show customers the types of patterns available. Not as formal as a standard sampler, this early 17th century book consists of fabric scraps which have been embroidered, and then sewn together and onto pages of parchment to form a book. The pattern samples are stitched in a variety of stitches, but several pages are devoted to designs worked in long-armed cross stitch and double running stitch with colored silks, and a few pages of cutwork, and bullion stitch worked in white thread.

Most of the patterns stitched in the sampler book appear to be Italian in design, but a few are similar to ones that appear in the German pattern books. Fig. 56, a diagonal band of flowers, worked in long-armed cross stitch over three threads, is similar to a pattern found in several of the pattern books (Fig. 57).

55. Booklet of Embroidery and Drawnwork, early 17th century, probably Portuguese, Metropolitan Museum of Art, Gift of Miss Mary Parsons, 1925, Accession Number: 25.92
56. Detail from Booklet of Embroidery and Drawnwork
57. Pattern from plate 140

Introduction

Metalwork

Textiles were not the only things which could be decorated with these patterns. This beautiful black and gold burgonet is a wonderful example of decorative, yet functional, metalwork. Made in Augsburg, Germany, between 1575 – 1600, it is decorated with a floral bud motif which is often seen in Hoffman's freestyle designs, and is similar to the middle design on plate 108 (Fig. 59).

58. Burgonet, Date: 1575 – 1600, The Metropolitan Museum of Art, Purchase, Clarence H. Mackay Gift, 1922, Accession Number: 22.168
59. Middle band of plate 108

German Modelbücher 1524 – 1556

Notes

1) **Neuper, Anna, and Nancy Spies**. Anna Neuper's Modelbuch: Early Sixteenth-Century Patterns for Weaving Brocaded Bands. Jarrettsville, MD: Arelate Studio, 2003.
2) **Lotz, Arthur**. Bibliographie Der Modelbücher. Leipzig: K.W. Hiersemann, 1963. p.35
3) **Speelberg, Femke** "Fashion and Virtue: Textile Patterns and the Print Revolution, 1520 – 1620", The Metropolitan Museum of Art Bulletin – Fall 2015 issue p.16
https://www.metmuseum.org/art/metpublications/Fashion_and_Virtue_Textile_Patterns_and_the_Print_Revolution_1520_1620
4) **Paganino, Alessandro** "Libro quarto", ca. 1532, Metropolitan Museum of Art, Accession Number:48.40(1-21) https://www.metmuseum.org/art/collection/search/354979 and Zoppino, Nicolò "Esemplario di lavori", 1529, Metropolitan Museum of Art, Rogers Fund, 1921, Acc. No:21.98(1-36) https://www.metmuseum.org/art/collection/search/349352
5) **Basse, Nikolaus, and Kathleen A. Epstein**. German Renaissance Patterns for Embroidery A Facsimile Copy of Nicolas Bassée's New Modelbuch of 1568. Austin: Curious Works Press, 1995.
6) **Lotz, Arthur**. Bibliographie Der Modelbücher ... Beschreibendes Verzeichnis Der Stick- Und Spitzenmusterbücher Des 16. Und 17. Jahrhunderts, Etc. 1933.
7) **Hough, Helen** "Early Modern Embroidery and Lace Pattern Books: 2017 Index" James G. Collins & Associates, Arlington, Texas, 2017
https://archive.org/details/Hough2017EarlyModernCEPR/
8) Examples of these books are held at Staatliche Museen zu Berlin, Kunstbibliothek Ein new modelbuch 1526, https://www.bildindex.de/document/obj14096873 ; F(urm oder modelbüchlein https://www.bildindex.de/document/obj14096872
9) **Egenolff, Christian** Modelbuch nehwens stickens und wirckens, 1555 Bayerische Staatsbibliothek: http://mdz-nbn-resolving.de/urn:nbn:de:bvb:12-bsb00084885-3
10) **Bombek, Marita, Gudrun Sporbeck, and Monika** Nürnberg. Kölner Bortenweberei im Mittelalter. Regensburg: Schnell & Steiner, 2012.
11) The Grove Encyclopedia of Medieval Art and Architecture, Volume 1, p.683
12) ID numbers A26874 and A26865
https://collections.museumoflondon.org.uk/online/object/90816.html
13) Title page from Paganini's "Il Burato: libro de recami"
https://archive.org/details/ilburatolibrodero0paga/page/n15

60. Hoffman 1556 f.IV , A lady with a tapestry loom

Freestyle Patterns
Plates 1 – 124

Freestyle Designs

1. Schönsperger 1524 f.1v, Schönsperger 1529 f.23r

German Modelbücher 1524 – 1556

2. Schönsperger 1524 f.2r, Schönsperger 1529 f.23v

Freestyle Designs

3. Schönsperger 1524 f.2v, Schönsperger 1529 f.20v

German Modelbücher 1524 – 1556

4. Schönsperger 1524 f.7r, Schönsperger 1529 f.22v

Freestyle Designs

5. Schönsperger 1524 f.7v, Schönsperger 1529 f.24r

German Modelbücher 1524 – 1556

6. Schönsperger 1524 f.8v, Schönsperger 1529 f.21v

Freestyle Designs

7. Schönsperger 1524 f.15v, Schönsperger 1529 f.22r

German Modelbücher 1524 – 1556

8. Schönsperger 1529 f.21r

Freestyle Designs

9. Schönsperger 1524 f.3r, Quentel 1529 f.3v, Quentel 1544 f.13r, Gülfferich 1553 f.10v

10. Schönsperger 1524 f.3v, Quentel 1529 f.5r, Quentel 1544 f.14r, Gülfferich 1553 f.6v

Freestyle Designs

11. Quentel 1529 f.4r, Quentel 1544 f.13v, Gülfferich 1553 f.12r

German Modelbücher 1524 – 1556

12. Quentel 1529 f.4v, Quentel 1544 f.14v, Gülfferich 1553 f.9v

Freestyle Designs

13. Quentel 1529 f.3r, Quentel 1544 f.12v, Gülfferich 1553 f.11r

German Modelbücher 1524 – 1556

14. Quentel 1532 f.3v, Quentel 1544 f.16v, Gülfferich 1553 f.11v

Freestyle Designs

15. Schönsperger 1524 f.4r, Quentel 1532 f.2r, Quentel 1544 f.15r, Gülfferich 1553 f.8r

German Modelbücher 1524 – 1556

16. Schönsperger 1524 f.4v, Quentel 1532 f.3r, Quentel 1544 f.16r, Gülfferich 1553 f.7v

Freestyle Designs

17. Schönsperger 1524 f.5r, Quentel 1532 f.4r, Gülfferich 1553 f.12v

German Modelbücher 1524 – 1556

18. Schönsperger 1524 f.5v, Quentel 1532 f.5r, Quentel 1544 f.17r, Gülfferich 1553 f.9r

Freestyle Designs

19. Schönsperger 1524 f.6r, Quentel 1532 f.1v, Quentel 1544 f.18r

20. Schönsperger 1524 f.9v, Quentel 1532 f.4v, Gülfferich 1553 f.8v

Freestyle Designs

21. Schönsperger 1524 f.10v, Quentel 1532 f.5v, Quentel 1544 f.17v, Gülfferich 1553 f.10r

German Modelbücher 1524 – 1556

22. Quentel 1532 f.2v, Quentel 1544 f.15v, Gülfferich 1553 f.7r

Freestyle Designs

23. Quentel 1544 f.6r, Gülfferich 1553 f.29r

German Modelbücher 1524 – 1556

24. Quentel 1544 f.8v, Gülfferich 1553 f.36v

Freestyle Designs

25. Quentel 1544 f.11v, Gülfferich 1553 f.28v

German Modelbücher 1524 – 1556

26. Egenolff 1535 f.5v

Freestyle Designs

27. Egenolff 1535 f.7r

German Modelbücher 1524 – 1556

28. Egenolff 1535 f.7v

Freestyle Designs

29. Egenolff 1535 f.8r

German Modelbücher 1524 – 1556

30. Egenolff 1535 f.5r

Freestyle Designs

31. Egenolff 1535 f.6v

German Modelbücher 1524 – 1556

32. Schönsperger 1524 f.12v, Quentel 1532 f.8v, Quentel 1544 f.19r

Freestyle Designs

33. Quentel 1532 f.10v, Gülfferich 1553 f.35v

34. Quentel 1532 f.11r

Freestyle Designs

35. Quentel 1532 f.11v, Gülfferich 1553 f.32r

German Modelbücher 1524 – 1556

36. Quentel 1532 f.12r

Freestyle Designs

37. *Quentel 1532 f.12v, Gülfferich 1553 f.32v*

German Modelbücher 1524 – 1556

38. Quentel 1532 f.6r

Freestyle Designs

39. Schönsperger 1524 f.11r, Quentel 1532 f.6v, Quentel 1544 f.18v, Gülfferich 1553 f.30r

German Modelbücher 1524 – 1556

40. Quentel 1532 f.7r, Quentel 1544 f.43v, Gülfferich 1553 f.27v

Freestyle Designs

41. Quentel 1532 f.7v

German Modelbücher 1524 – 1556

42. Schönsperger 1524 f.6v, Quentel 1532 f.8r, Quentel 1544 f.19v, Egenolff 1535 f.6r, Gülfferich 1553 f.30v

Freestyle Designs

43. Quentel 1532 f.9r

German Modelbücher 1524 – 1556

44. Quentel 1532 f.9v, Quentel 1544 f.43r, Gülfferich 1553 f.31r

Freestyle Designs

45. Quentel 1529 f.6r, Quentel 1544 f.48v, Gülfferich 1553 f.27r

46. Quentel 1544 f.49r, Güfferich 1553 f.36r

Freestyle Designs

47. Quentel 1544 f.49v

48. Quentel 1544 f.50v, Güfferich 1553 f.34r

Freestyle Designs

49. Quentel 1544 f.51r, Güfferich 1553 f.31v

50. Quentel 1544 f.10r, Güfferich 1553 f.33v

Freestyle Designs

51. Quentel 1544 f.48r, Güfferich 1553 f.33r

52. Egenolff 1535 f.2r

Freestyle Designs

53. *Egenolff 1535 f.2v*

German Modelbücher 1524 – 1556

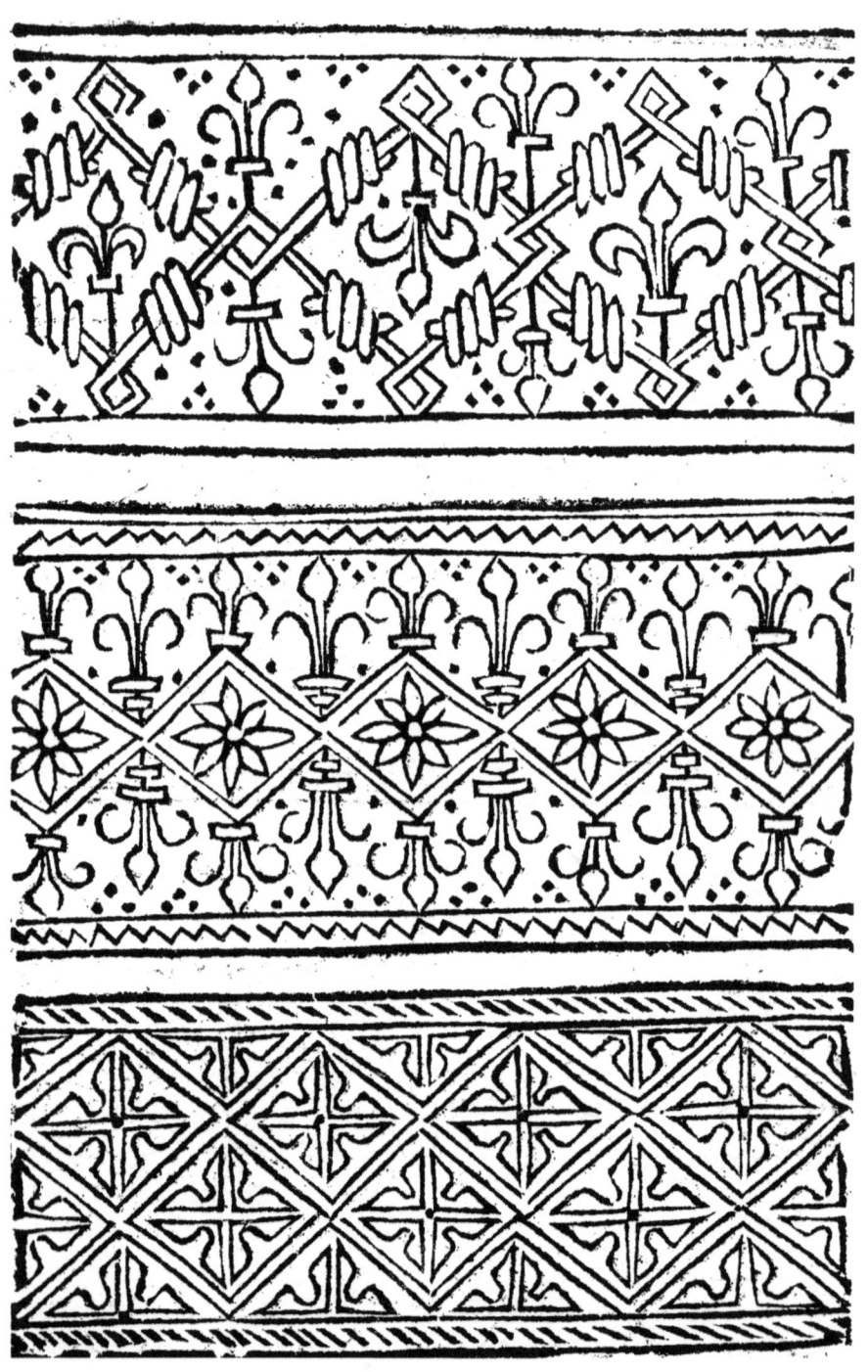

54. Egenolff 1535 f.3r

Freestyle Designs

55. *Egenolff 1535 f.3v*

56. Egenolff 1535 f.10r

Freestyle Designs

57. *Egenolff 1535 f.10v*

58. Egenolff 1535 f.11r

59. Egenolff 1535 f.IIv

German Modelbücher 1524 – 1556

60. Egenolff 1535 f.12r

Freestyle Designs

61. Egenolff 1535 f.12v

62. Egenolff 1535 f.9v

Freestyle Designs

63. *Quentel 1544 f.2r, Gülfferich 1553 f.3r*

German Modelbücher 1524 – 1556

64. Quentel 1544 f.2v, Gülfferich 1553 f.2v

Freestyle Designs

65. Quentel 1544 f.3r, Gülfferich 1553 f.3v, Hoffman 1556 f.12r

German Modelbücher 1524 – 1556

66. Quentel 1544 f.3v, Gülfferich 1553 f.6r, Hoffman 1556 f.12v

Freestyle Designs

67. Quentel 1544 f.4r, Gülfferich 1553 f.5r

German Modelbücher 1524 – 1556

68. Quentel 1544 f.4v, Gülfferich 1553 f.5v

Freestyle Designs

69. Quentel 1544 f.5r, Gülfferich 1553 f.4v

German Modelbücher 1524 – 1556

70. Quentel 1544 f.5v, Gülfferich 1553 f.2r

Freestyle Designs

71. Quentel 1544 f.12r, Gülfferich 1553 f.4r

72. Hoffman 1556 f.3r

Freestyle Designs

73. Hoffman 1556 f.3v

German Modelbücher 1524 – 1556

74. Hoffman 1556 f.4r

Freestyle Designs

75. *Hoffman 1556 f.4v*

German Modelbücher 1524 – 1556

76. Hoffman 1556 f.5r

Freestyle Designs

77. Hoffman 1556 f.5v

German Modelbücher 1524 – 1556

78. Hoffman 1556 f.6r

Freestyle Designs

79. Hoffman 1556 f.6v

German Modelbücher 1524 – 1556

80. Hoffman 1556 f.7r

Freestyle Designs

81. Hoffman 1556 f.7v

German Modelbücher 1524 – 1556

82. Hoffman 1556 f.8r

Freestyle Designs

83. Hoffman 1556 f.8v

German Modelbücher 1524 – 1556

84. Hoffman 1556 f.9r

Freestyle Designs

85. Hoffman 1556 f.9v

German Modelbücher 1524 – 1556

86. Hoffman 1556 f.10r

Freestyle Designs

87. *Hoffman 1556 f.10v*

German Modelbücher 1524 – 1556

88. Hoffman 1556 f.11r

Freestyle Designs

89. *Hoffman 1556 f.11v*
   (See plates 65 and 66 for Hoffman 1556 f.12r and f.12v)

German Modelbücher 1524 – 1556

90. Hoffman 1556 f.13r

Freestyle Designs

91. Hoffman 1556 f.13v

German Modelbücher 1524 – 1556

92. Hoffman 1556 f.14r

Freestyle Designs

93. *Gülfferich 1553 f.13v*

94. Gülfferich 1553 f.13r

Freestyle Designs

95. Gülfferich 1553 f.14v

German Modelbücher 1524 – 1556

96. Gülfferich 1553 f.14r

Freestyle Designs

97. Gülfferich 1553 f.15v

98. Gülfferich 1553 f.15r

Freestyle Designs

99. Gülfferich 1553 f.16r

German Modelbücher 1524 – 1556

100. Hoffman 1556 f.14v

Freestyle Designs

101. Hoffman 1556 f.15r

German Modelbücher 1524 – 1556

102. Hoffman 1556 f.15v

Freestyle Designs

103. *Hoffman 1556 f.16r*

104. Hoffman 1556 f.16v

Freestyle Designs

105. Hoffman 1556 f.17r

German Modelbücher 1524 – 1556

106. Hoffman 1556 f.17v

Freestyle Designs

107. Hoffman 1556 f.18r

108. Hoffman 1556 f.18v

Freestyle Designs

109. Hoffman 1556 f.19r

German Modelbücher 1524 – 1556

110. Hoffman 1556 f.19v

Freestyle Designs

III. Hoffman 1556 f.20r

German Modelbücher 1524 – 1556

112. Hoffman 1556 f.20v

Freestyle Designs

113. Hoffman 1556 f.21r

German Modelbücher 1524 – 1556

114. Hoffman 1556 f.21v

Freestyle Designs

115. Hoffman 1556 f.22r

116. Hoffman 1556 f.22v

Freestyle Designs

117. Hoffman 1556 f.23r

118. Hoffman 1556 f.23v

Freestyle Designs

119. Hoffman 1556 f.24r

German Modelbücher 1524 – 1556

120. Hoffman 1556 f.24v

Freestyle Designs

121. Hoffman 1556 f.25r

122. Hoffman 1556 f.25v

Freestyle Designs

123. Hoffman 1556 f.26r

German Modelbücher 1524 – 1556

124. Hoffman 1556 f.26v

Charted Patterns
Plates 125 – 200

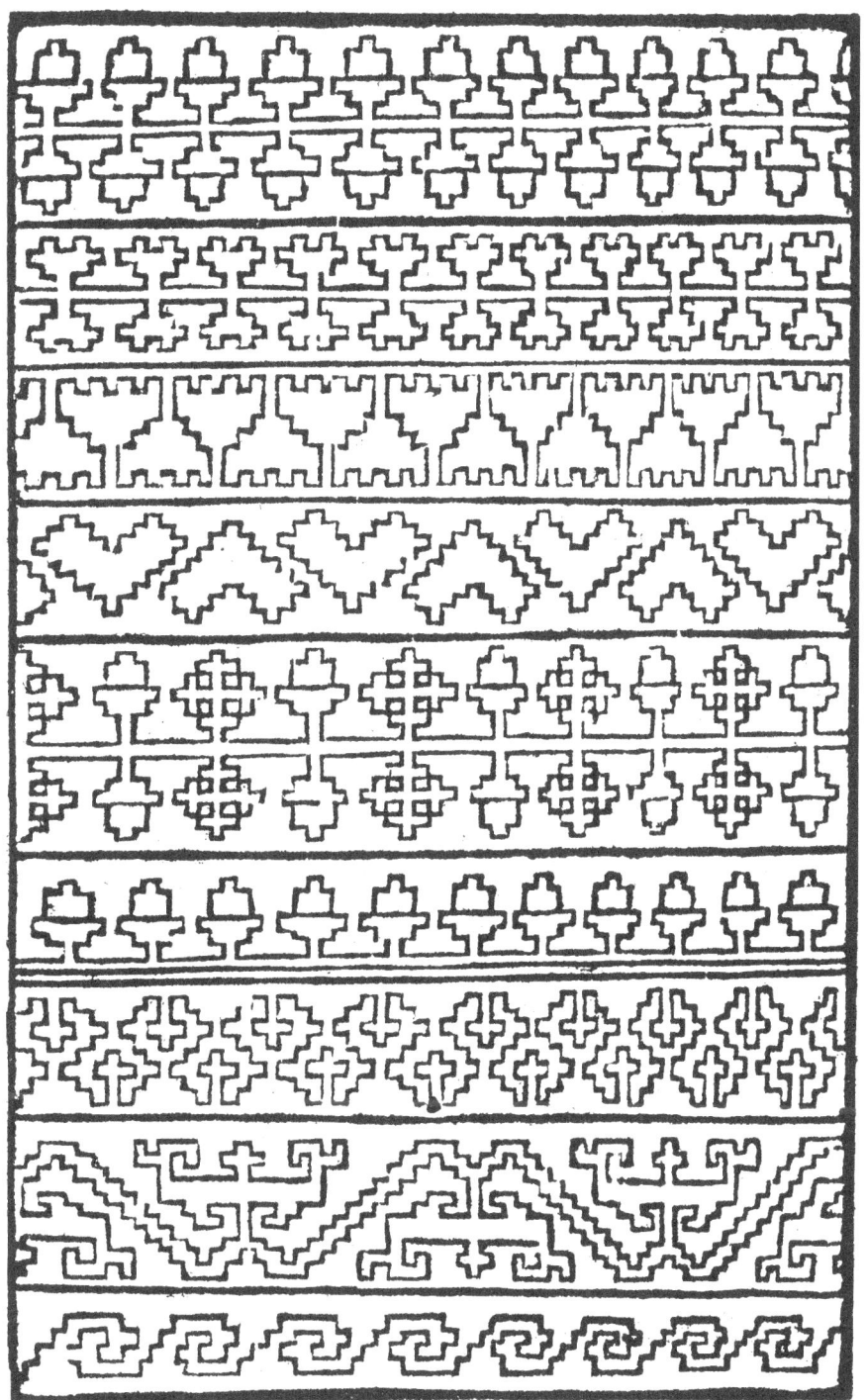

125. Schönsperger 1529 f.18v, Quentel 1529 f.8r, Quentel 1544 f.47r, Gülfferich 1553 f.25v

German Modelbücher 1524 – 1556

126. Schönsperger 1529 f.17r

Charted Designs

127. Quentel 1529 f.6v, Quentel 1544 f.45v, Gülfferich 1553 f.25r

German Modelbücher 1524 – 1556

128. Schönsperger 1529 f.18r

Charted Designs

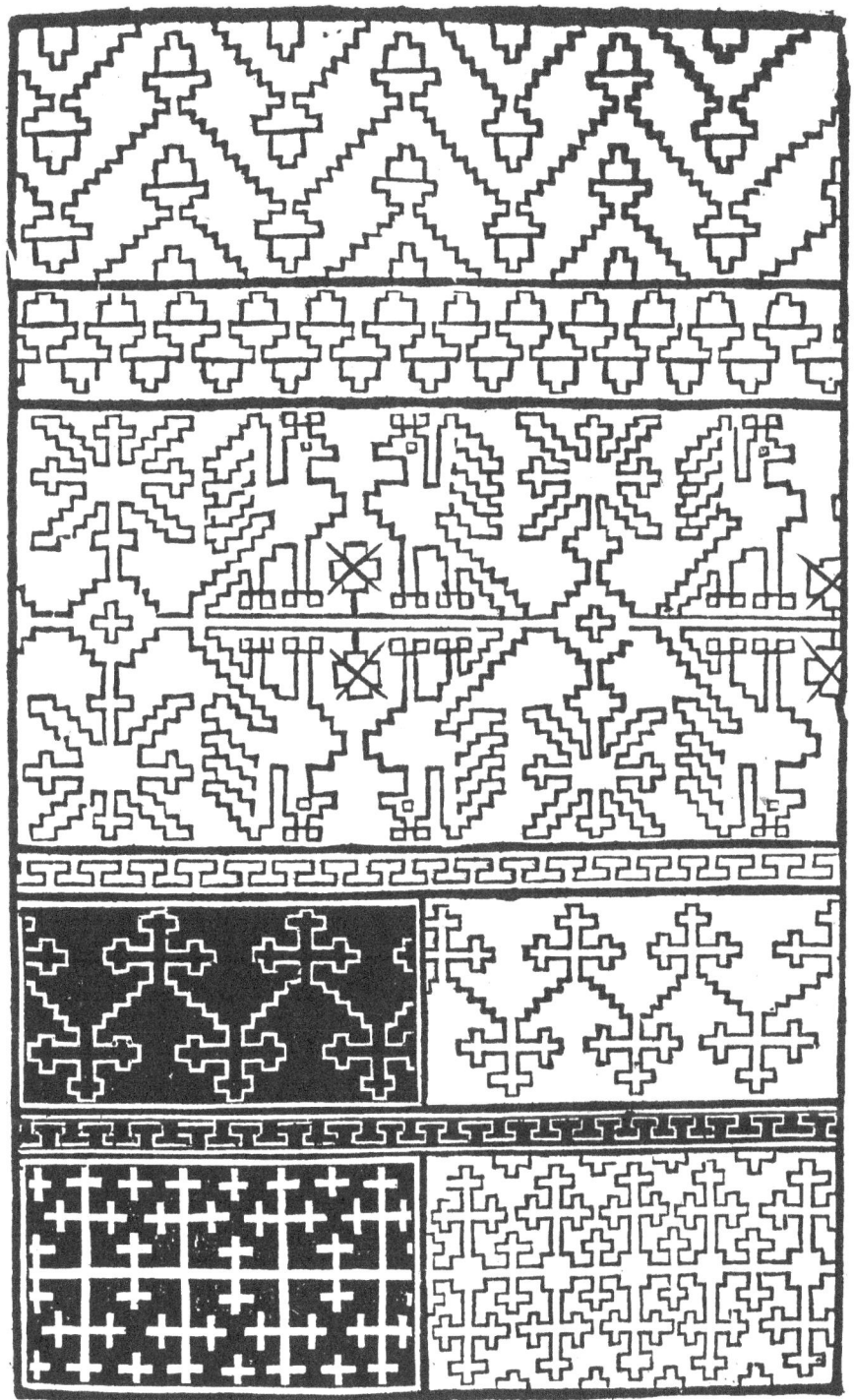

129. Quentel 1529 f.5v, Quentel 1544 f.45r, Gülfferich 1553 f.26v

130. Schönsperger 1529 f.19r

Charted Designs

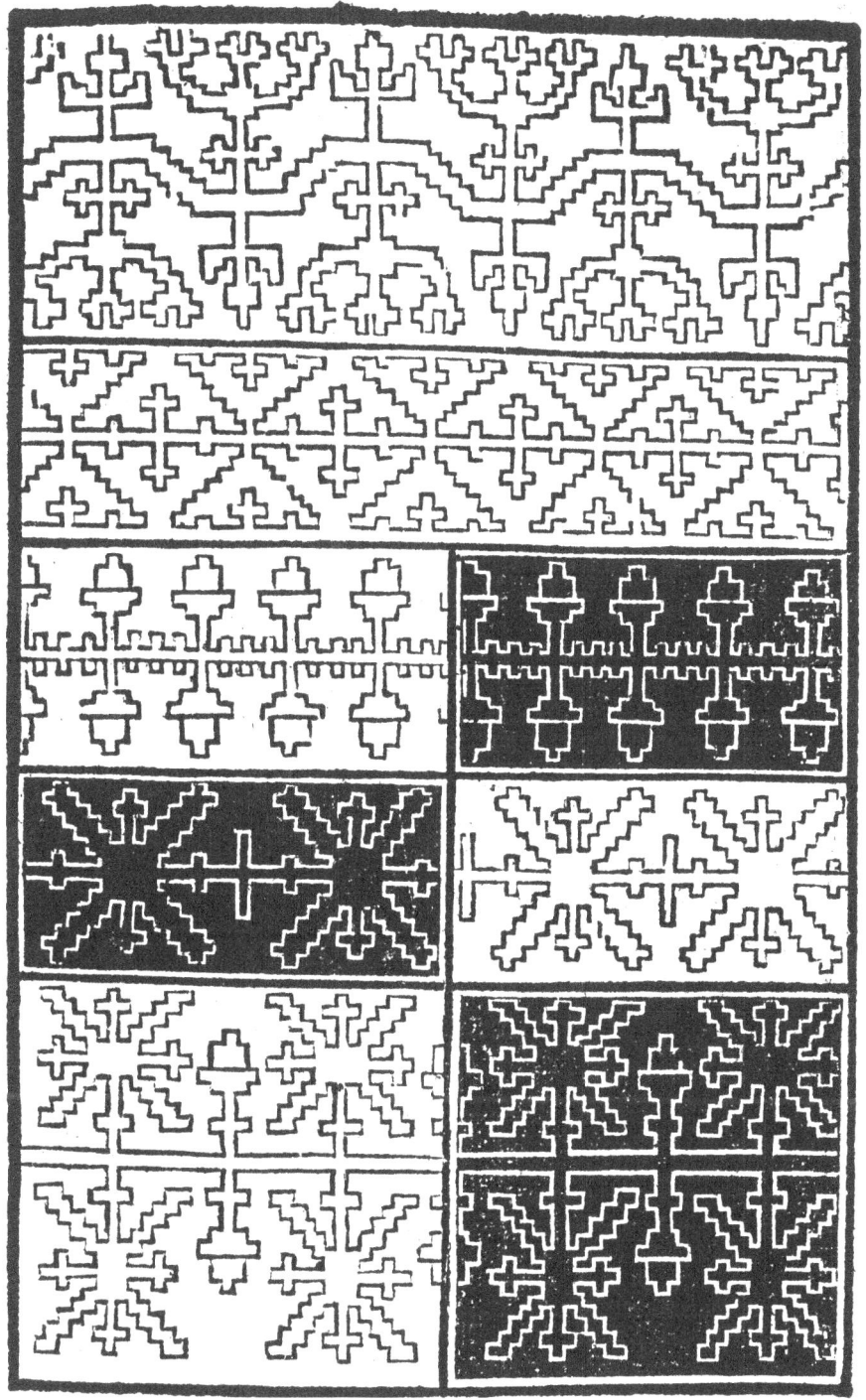

131. Quentel 1529 f.7r, Quentel 1544 f.46r, Gülfferich 1553 f.24v

132. Schönsperger 1529 f.19v

Charted Designs

133. Quentel 1529 f.7v, Quentel 1544 f.46v, Gülfferich 1553 f.26r

German Modelbücher 1524 – 1556

134. Schönsperger 1529 f.20r, Quentel 1529 f.9r, Quentel 1544 f.47v, Gülfferich 1553 f.35r

Charted Designs

135. Schönsperger 1529 f.12r, Quentel 1529 f.8v

German Modelbücher 1524 – 1556

136. Egenolff 1535 f.4v

Charted Designs

137. Quentel 1544 f.44v, Gülfferich 1553 f.29v

German Modelbücher 1524 – 1556

138. Quentel 1544 f.44r, Gülfferich 1553 f.28r

Charted Designs

139. Schönsperger 1529 f.2r, Quentel 1529 f.23r, Quentel 1544 f.36r, Gülfferich 1553 f.18r

German Modelbücher 1524 – 1556

140. Schönsperger 1529 f.6v, Quentel 1529 f.21v, Quentel 1544 f.35v, Gülfferich 1553 f.19v

Charted Designs

141. Schönsperger 1529 f.5r, Quentel 1529 f.21r, Quentel 1544 f.34r, Gülfferich 1553 f.19r

German Modelbücher 1524 – 1556

142. Schönsperger 1529 f.7r, Quentel 1529 f.12v, Quentel 1544 f.26r, Gülfferich 1553 f.22r

Charted Designs

143. Schönsperger 1529 f.3r, Quentel 1529 f.11r, Quentel 1544 f.24v

German Modelbücher 1524 – 1556

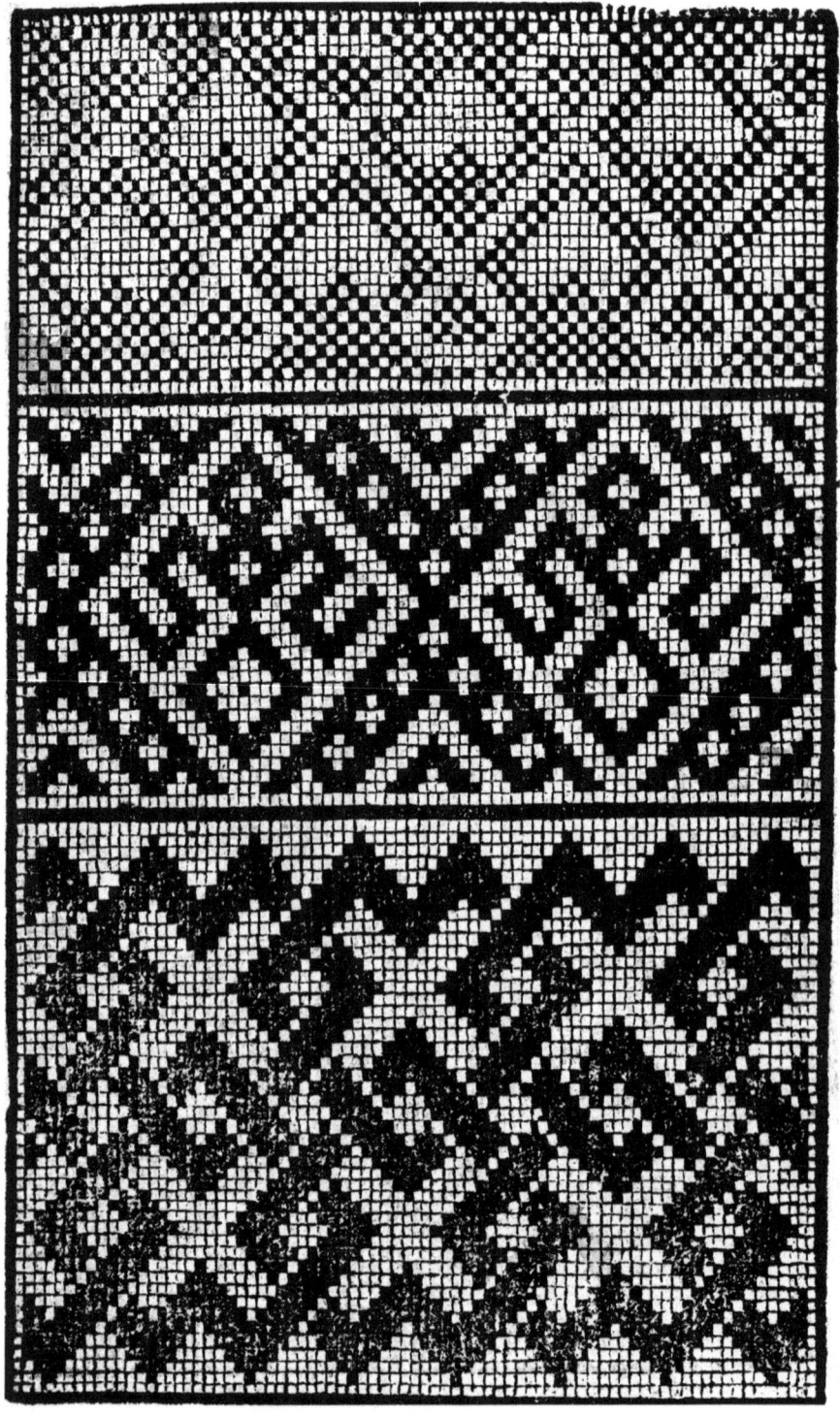

144. Schönsperger 1529 f.14v, Quentel 1529 f.20v, Quentel 1544 f.34v

Charted Designs

145. Schönsperger 1529 f.4r, Quentel 1529 f.11v, Quentel 1544 f.25v

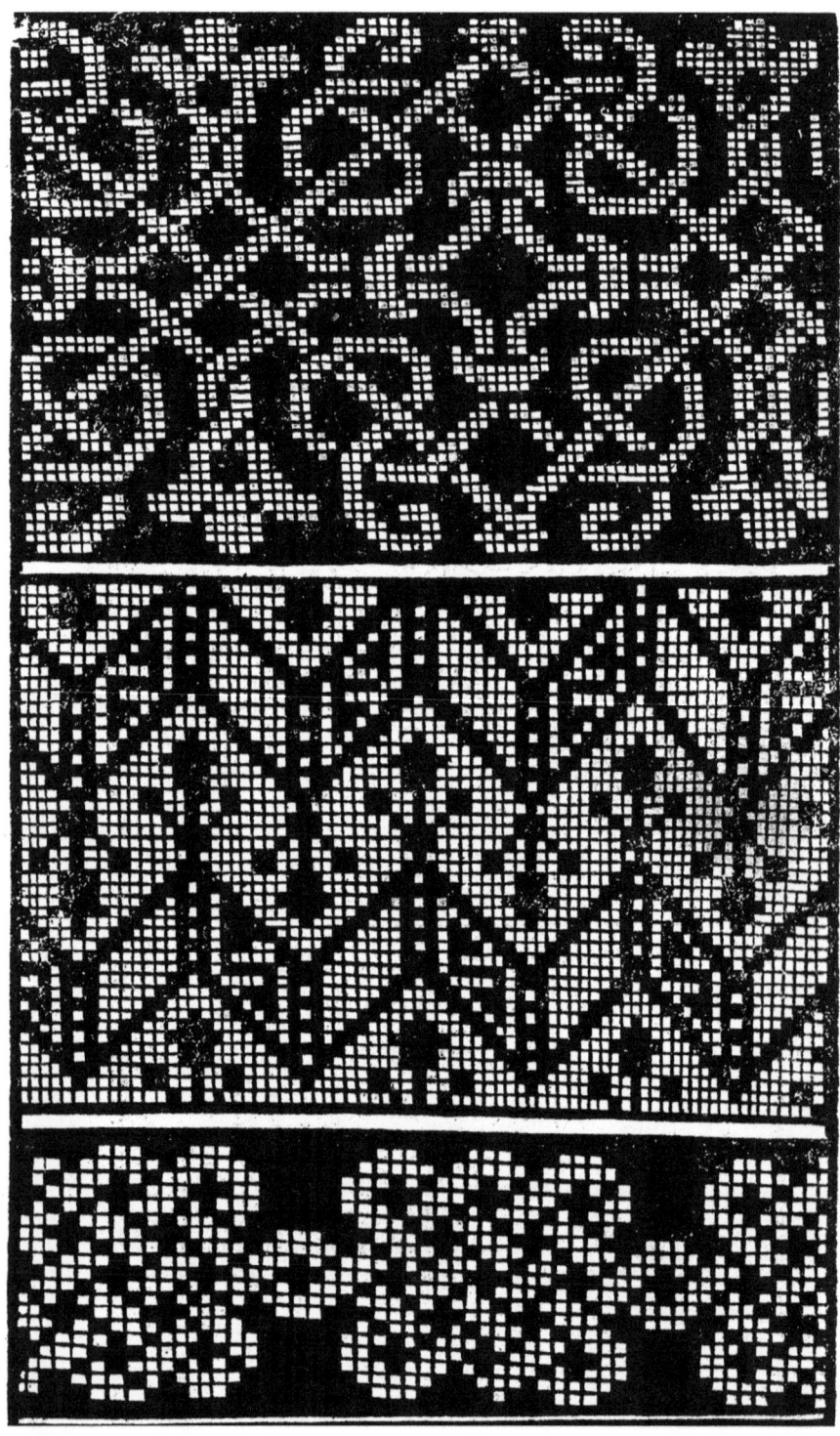

146. Quentel 1544 f.11r

Charted Designs

147. Quentel 1544 f.9r, Gülfferich 1553 f.21r

148. Schönsperger 1529 f.14r, Quentel 1529 f.17r, Quentel 1544 f.30v

Charted Designs

149. Schönsperger 1529 f.9r, Quentel 1529 f.10v, Quentel 1544 f.24r

German Modelbücher 1524 – 1556

150. Schönsperger 1529 f.12v, Quentel 1529 f.20r, Quentel 1544 f.33r

Charted Designs

151. Schönsperger 1529 f.10v, Quentel 1529 f.14r, Quentel 1544 f.27v, Gülfferich 1553 f.17v

German Modelbücher 1524 – 1556

152. Schönsperger 1529 f.10r, Quentel 1529 f.23v, Quentel 1544 f.37r, Gülfferich 1553 f.22v

Charted Designs

153. Schönsperger 1529 f.11r, Quentel 1529 f.18r, Quentel 1544 f.31v, Gülfferich 1553 f.21v

German Modelbücher 1524 – 1556

154. Quentel 1529 f.9v, Quentel 1544 f.50r

Charted Designs

155. Quentel 1532 f.16r, Quentel 1544 f.21r

156. Quentel 1532 f.13v, Quentel 1544 f.20v

Charted Designs

157. Quentel 1544 f.40v

German Modelbücher 1524 – 1556

158. Quentel 1529 f.10r, Quentel 1544 f.20r

Charted Designs

159. Quentel 1544 f.42r

German Modelbücher 1524 – 1556

160. Quentel 1544 f.39r

Charted Designs

161. Quentel 1544 f.41v

German Modelbücher 1524 – 1556

162. Quentel 1532 f.16v, Quentel 1544 f.22r

Charted Designs

163. Quentel 1544 f.38v

164. Quentel 1544 f.42v

Charted Designs

165. Quentel 1532 f.14v, Quentel 1544 f.23r

German Modelbücher 1524 – 1556

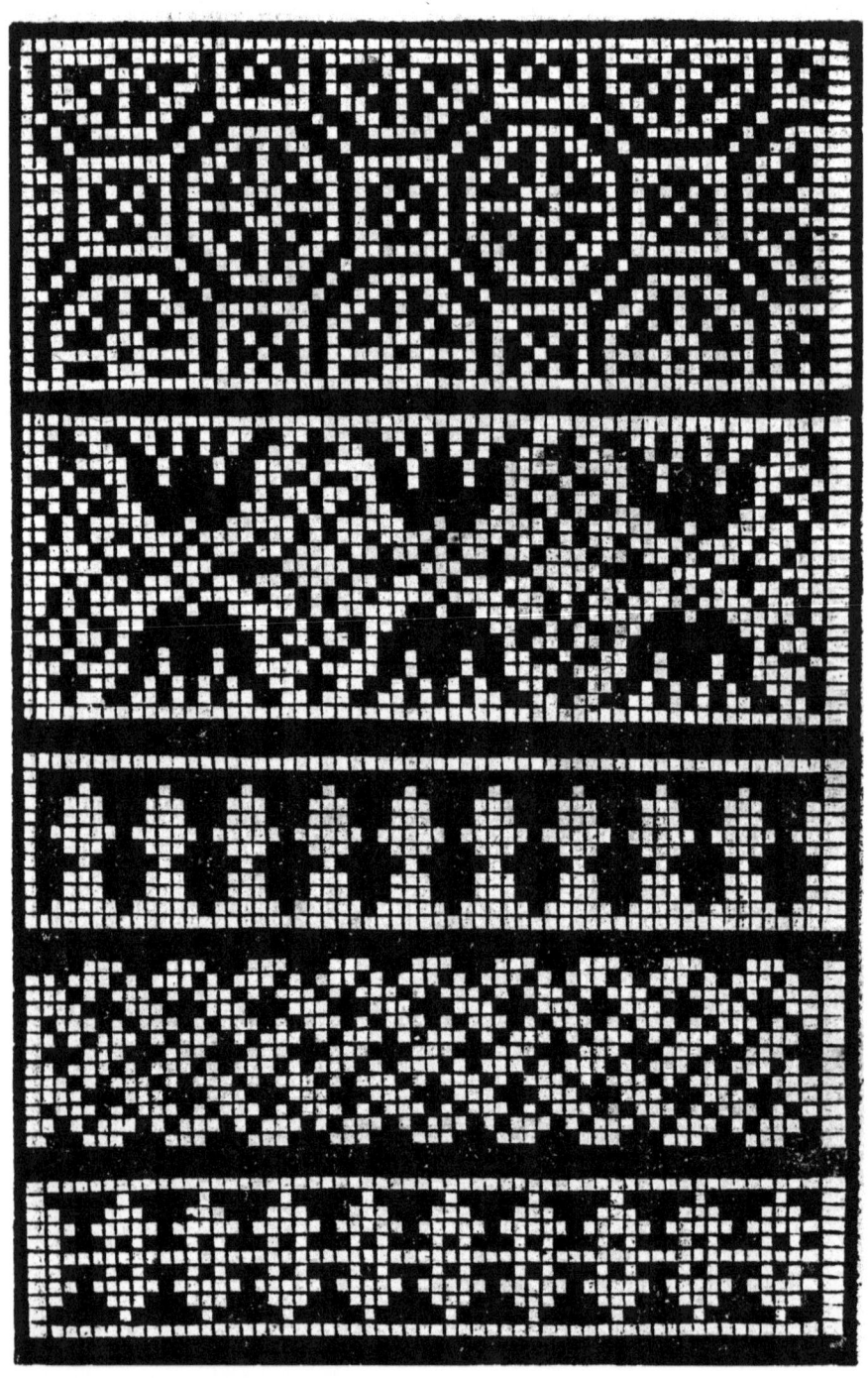

166. Quentel 1532 f.15v, Quentel 1544 f.23v

Charted Designs

167. Quentel 1544 f.40r

German Modelbücher 1524 – 1556

168. Quentel 1544 f.38r

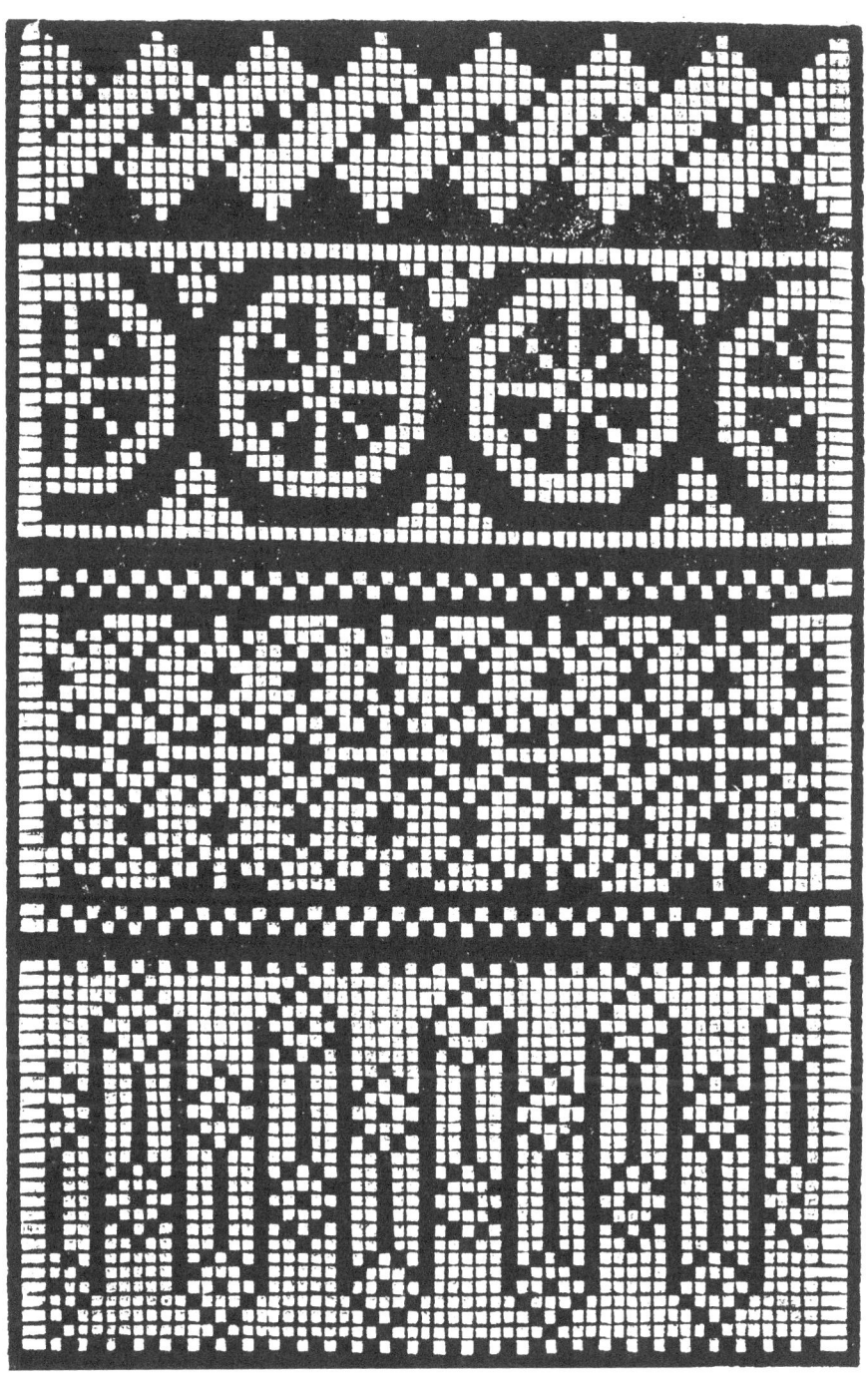

169. Quentel 1532 f.14r, Quentel 1544 f.22v

German Modelbücher 1524 – 1556

170. Quentel 1544 f.21v

Charted Designs

171. Quentel 1544 f.10v

172. Quentel 1532 f.13r, Quentel 1544 f.37v

Charted Designs

173. Quentel 1544 f.41r

German Modelbücher 1524 – 1556

174. Schönsperger 1529 f.3v, Quentel 1529 f.22v, Quentel 1544 f.36v, Gülfferich 1553 f.20r

Charted Designs

175. Schönsperger 1529 f.6r, Quentel 1529 f.22r, Quentel 1544 f.35r

German Modelbücher 1524 – 1556

176. Schönsperger 1529 f.5v, Quentel 1529 f.12r, Quentel 1544 f.25r

Charted Designs

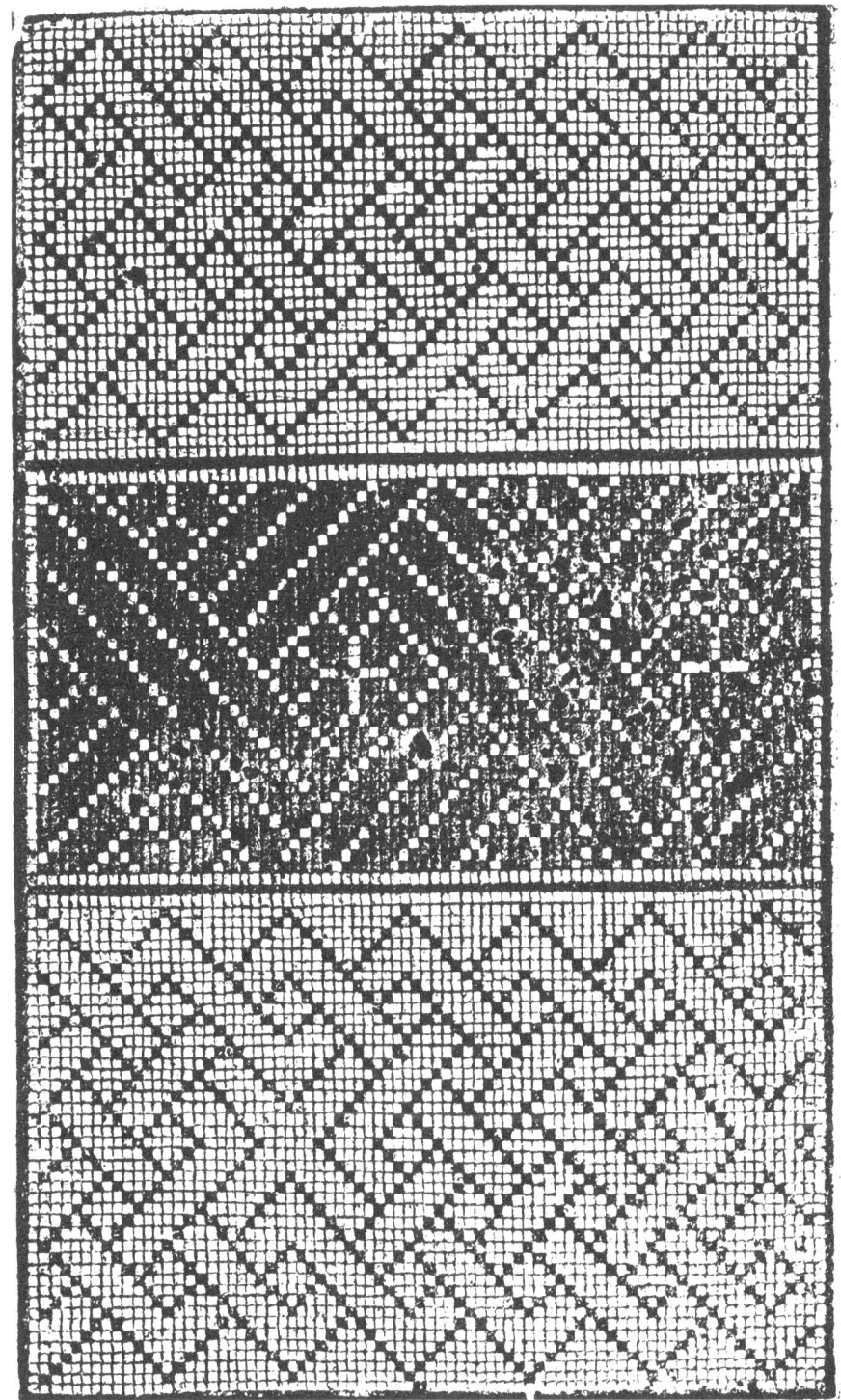

177. Schönsperger 1529 f.13r, Quentel 1529 f.16r, Quentel 1544 f.29r

German Modelbücher 1524 – 1556

178. Schönsperger 1529 f.16r, Quentel 1529 f.14v, Quentel 1544 f.28v

Charted Designs

179. Schönsperger 1529 f.16v, Quentel 1529 f.16v, Quentel 1544 f.30r, Gülfferich 1553 f.18v

German Modelbücher 1524 – 1556

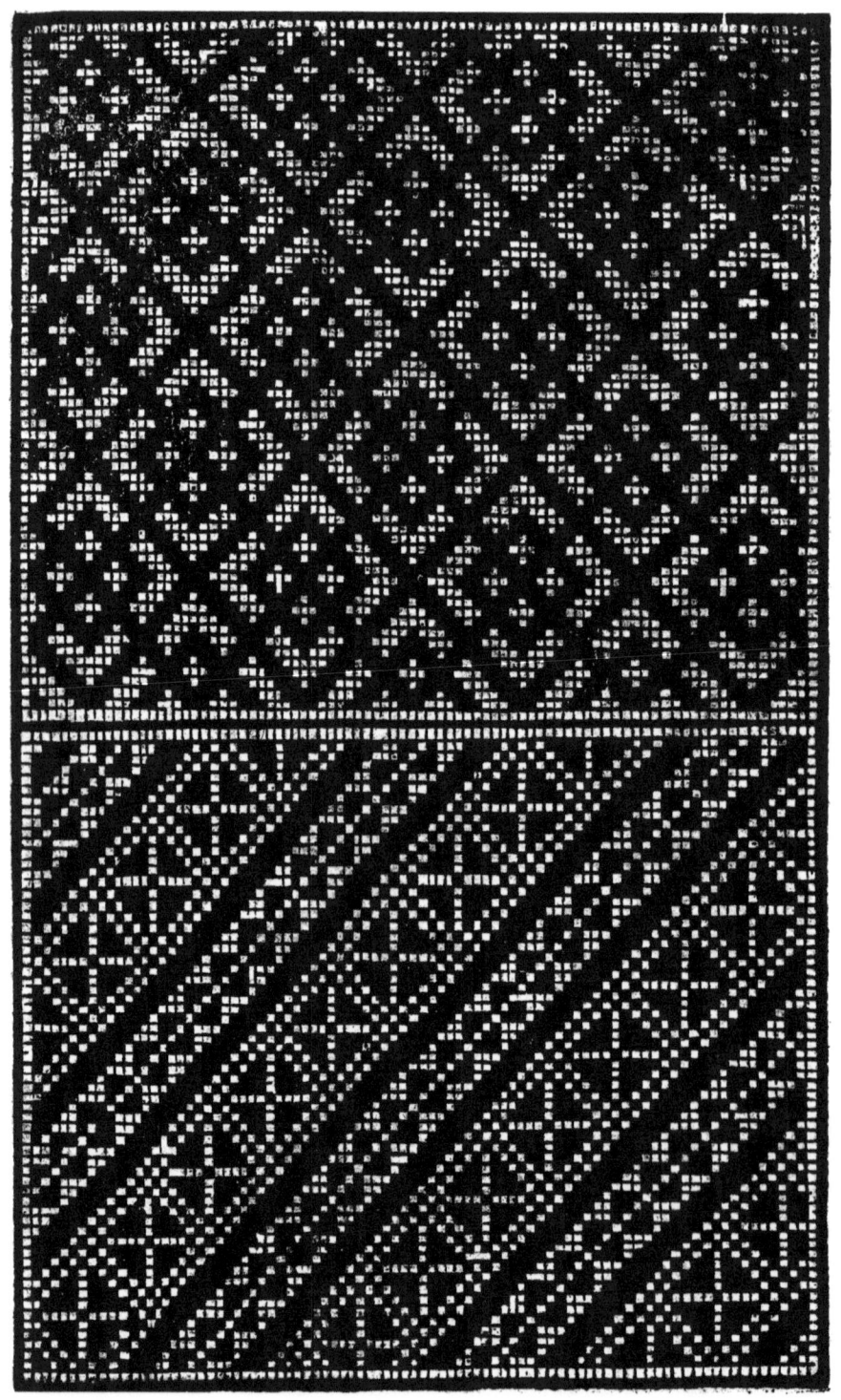

180. Quentel 1529 f.17v, Quentel 1544 f.31r

Charted Designs

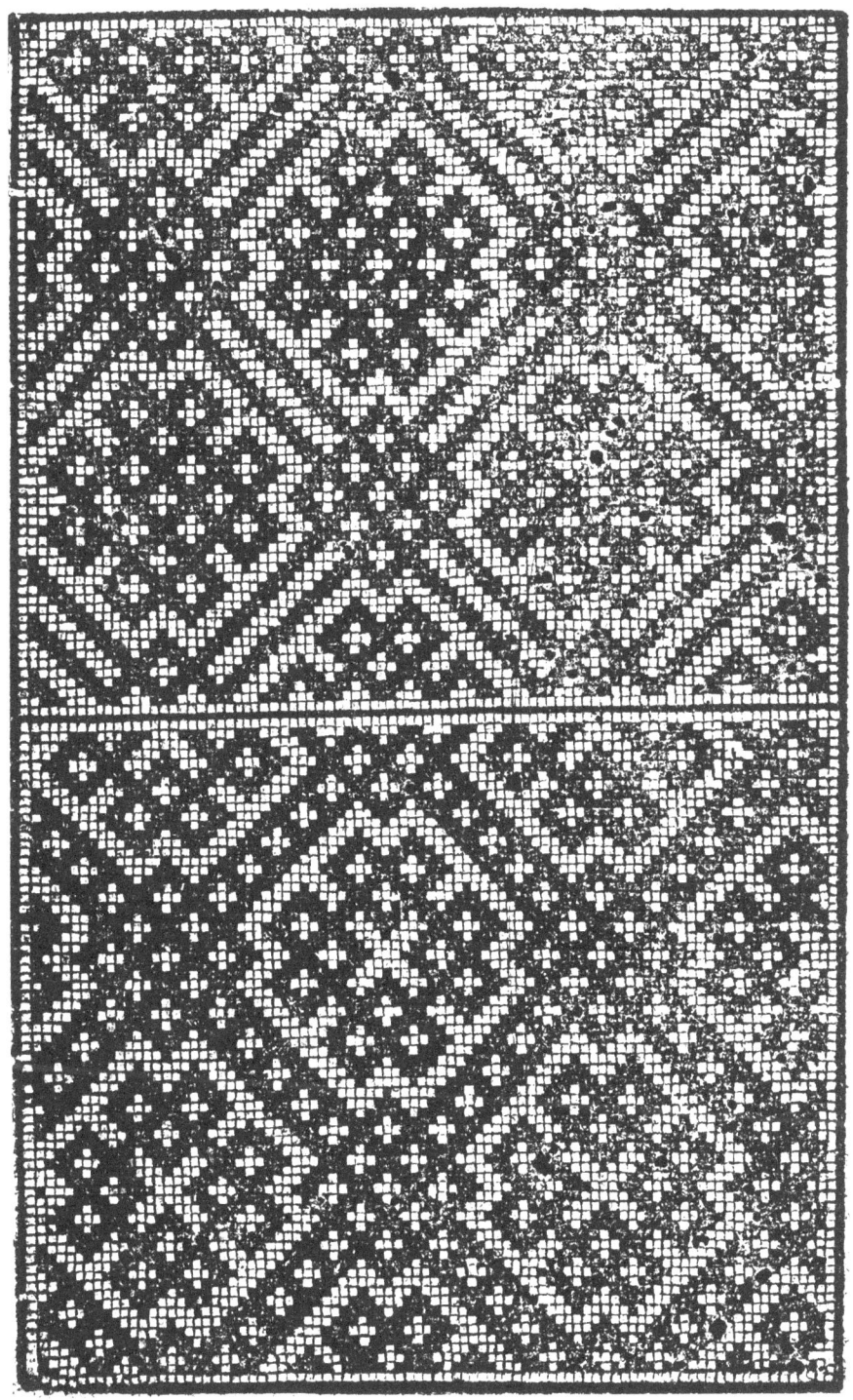

181. Schönsperger 1529 f.11v, Quentel 1529 f.13r, Quentel 1544 f.26r, Gülfferich 1553 f.16v

German Modelbücher 1524 – 1556

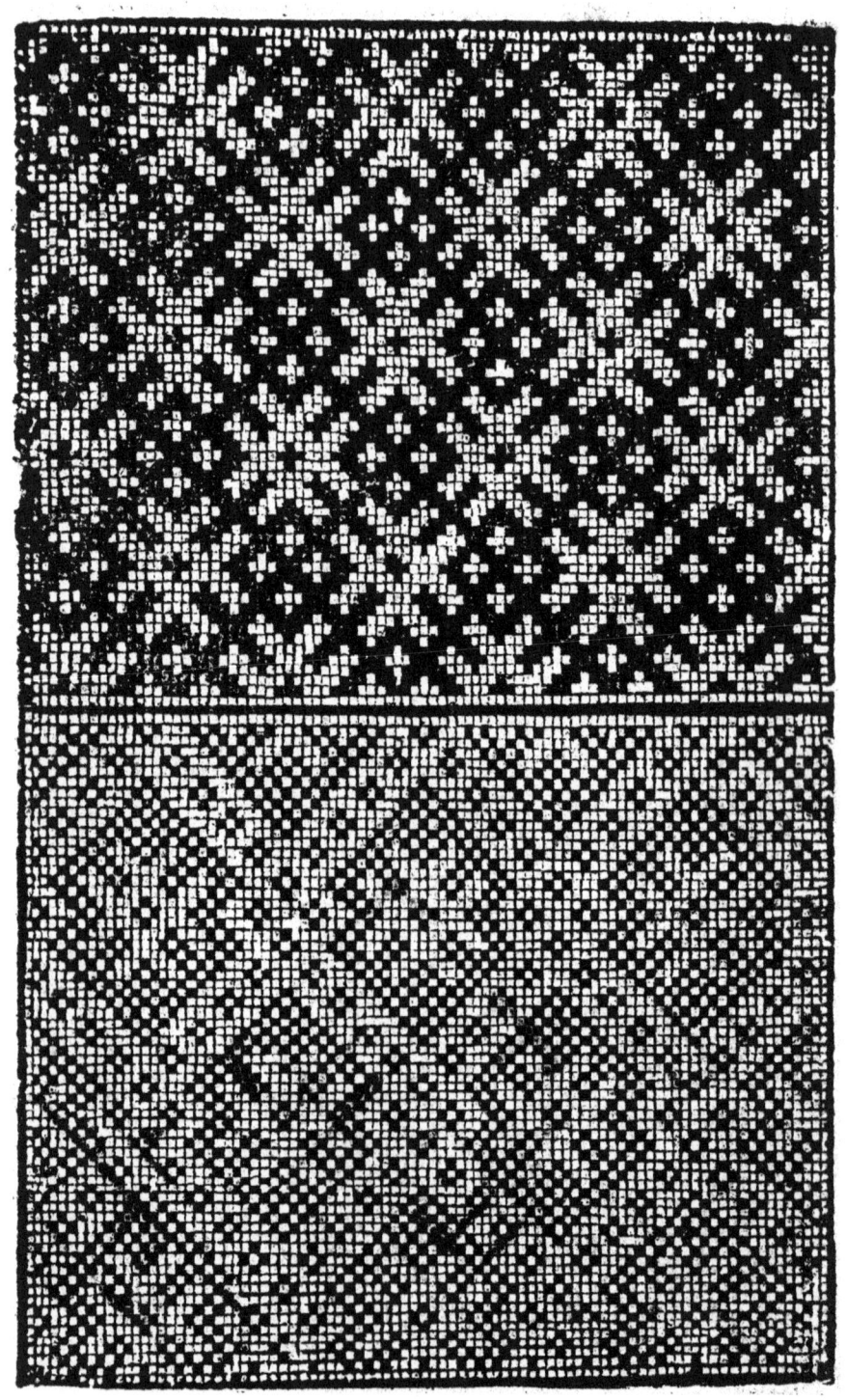

182. Schönsperger 1529 f.7v, Quentel 1529 f.18v, Quentel 1544 f.32r

Charted Designs

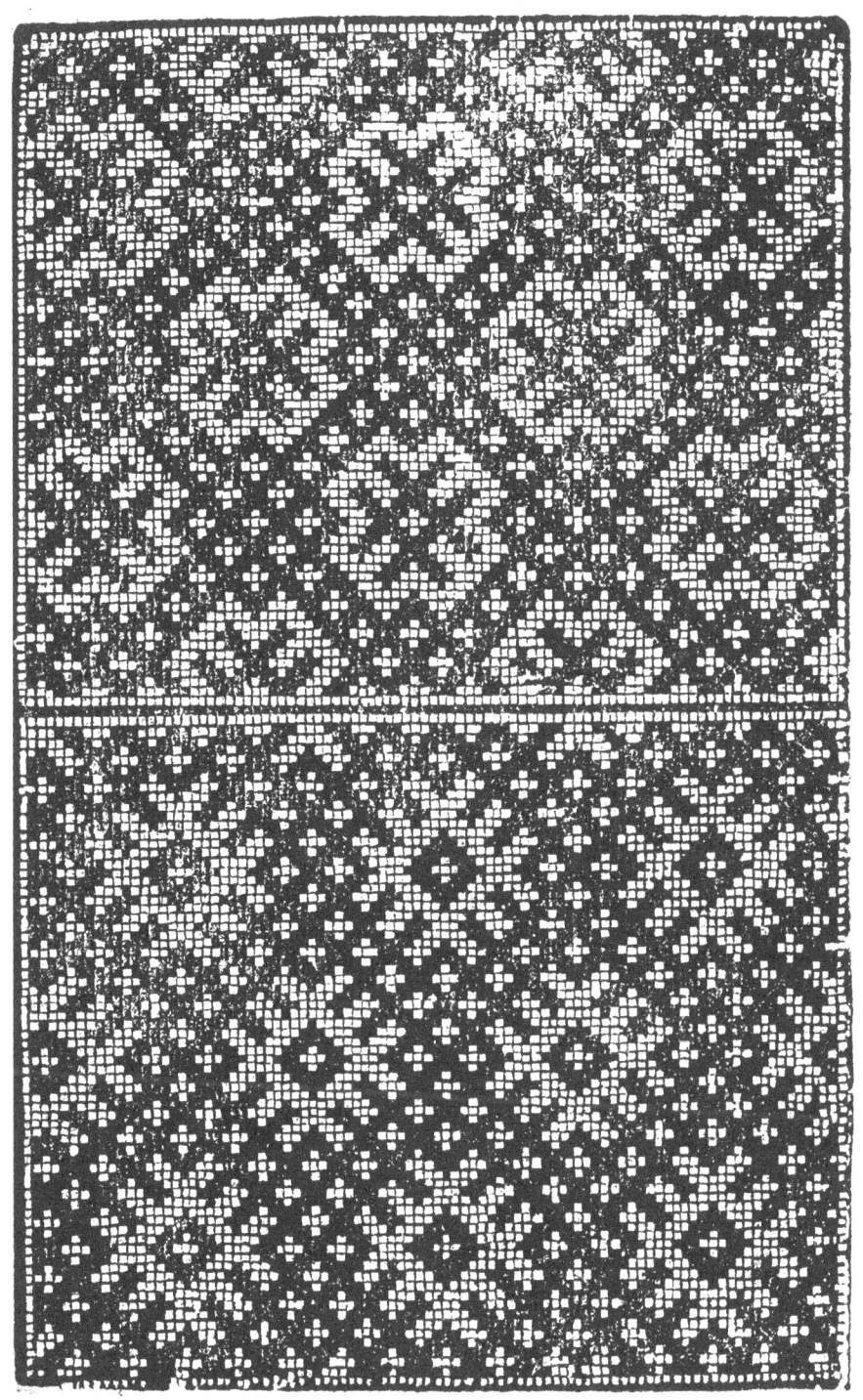

183. Schönsperger 1529 f.2v, Quentel 1529 f.15r, Quentel 1544 f.29r, Gülfferich 1553 f.23r

German Modelbücher 1524 – 1556

184. Schönsperger 1529 f.13v, Quentel 1529 f.15v, Quentel 1544 f.28r

Charted Designs

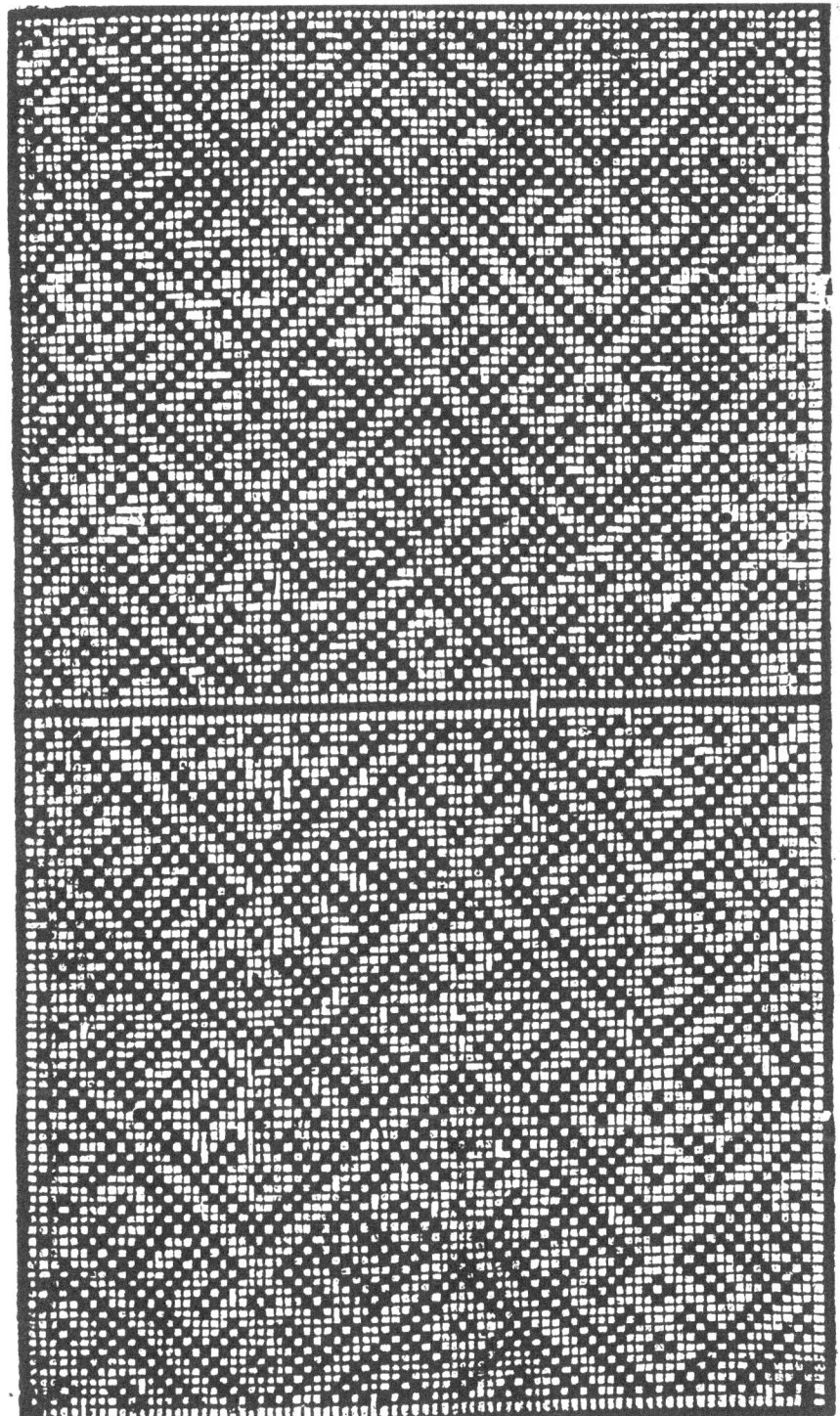

185. Quentel 1529 f.19v, Quentel 1544 f.33v

German Modelbücher 1524 – 1556

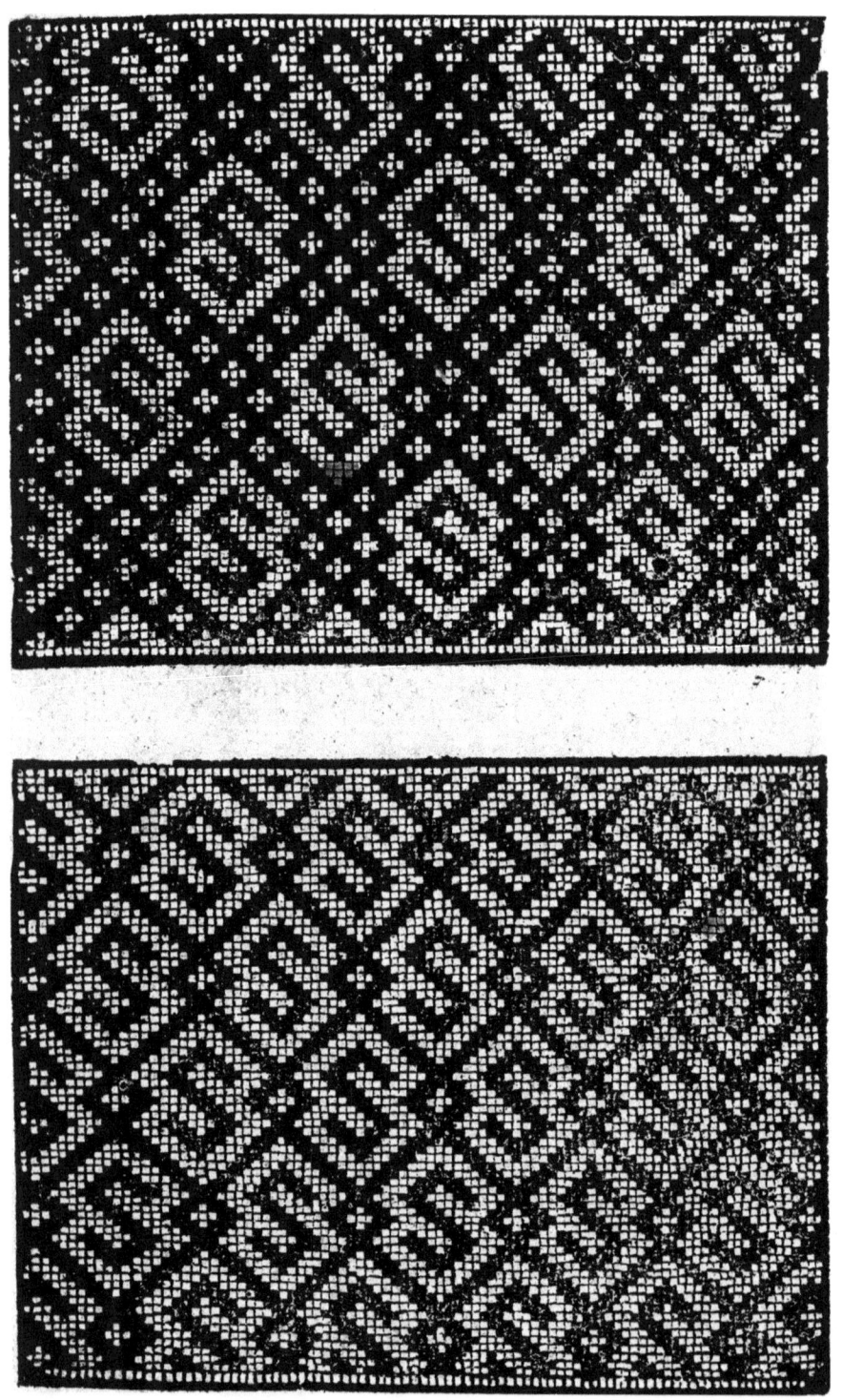

186. Schönsperger 1529 f.8r, Quentel 1529 f.19v, Quentel 1544 f.32v, Gülfferich 1553 f.24r

Charted Designs

187. Schönsperger 1529 f.4v, Quentel 1529 f.13v, Quentel 1544 f.27r, Gülfferich 1553 f.17r

German Modelbücher 1524 – 1556

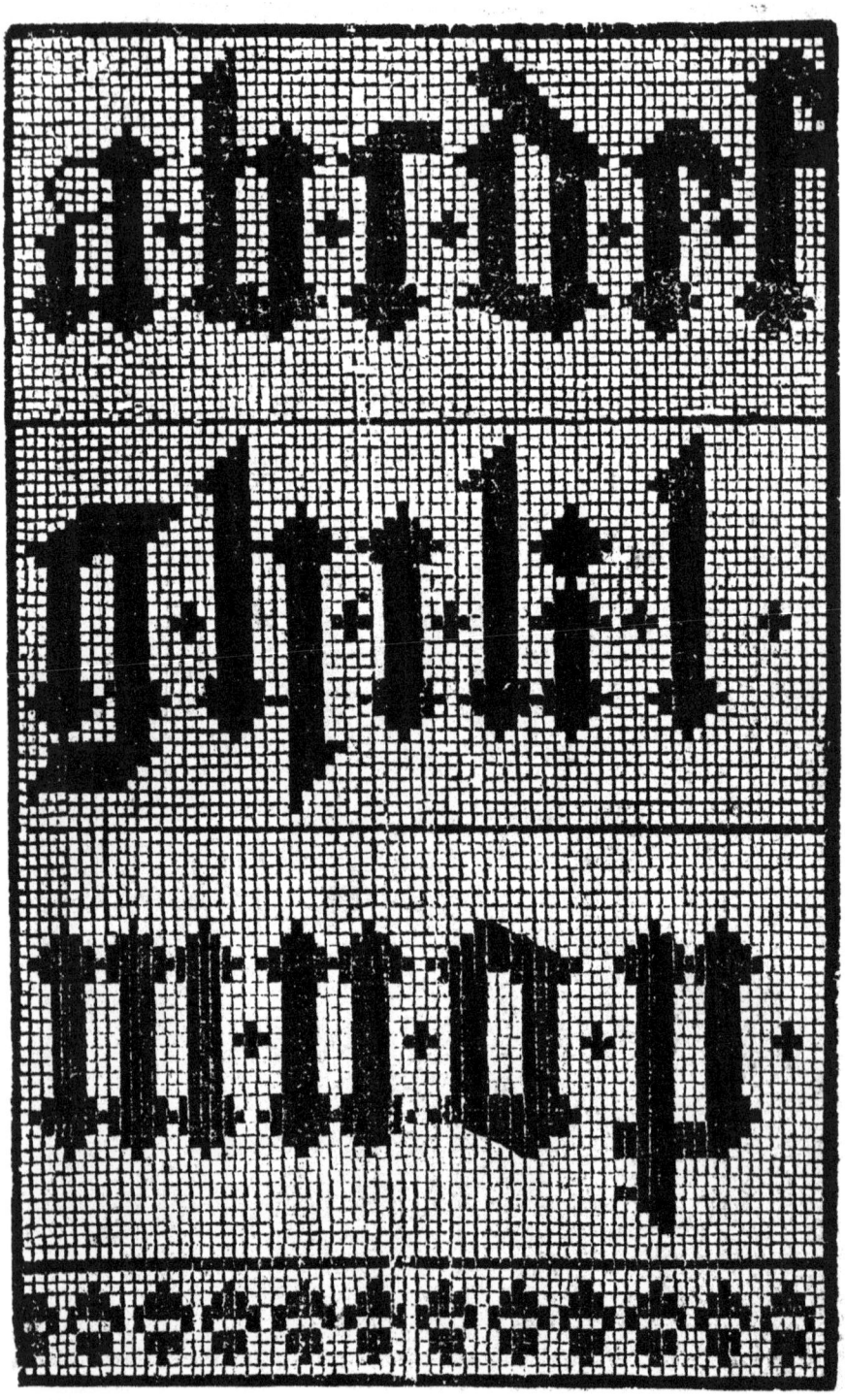

188. Schönsperger 1529 f.15r, Quentel 1529 f.24r

Charted Designs

189. Schönsperger 1529 f.15v, Quentel 1529 f.24v

German Modelbücher 1524 – 1556

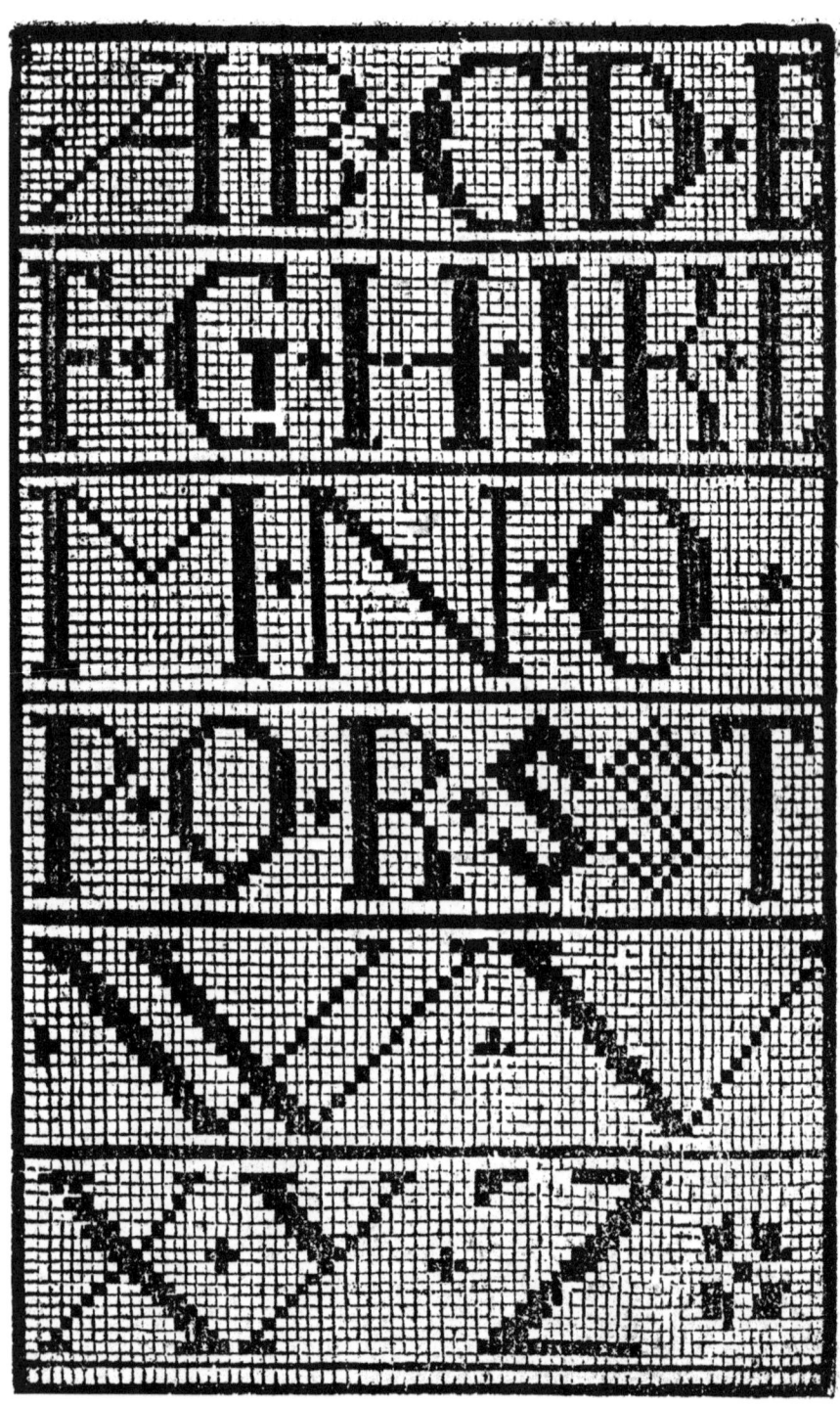

190. Schönsperger 1529 f.17v, Quentel 1529 f.25r

Charted Designs

191. Quentel 1544 f.6v

German Modelbücher 1524 – 1556

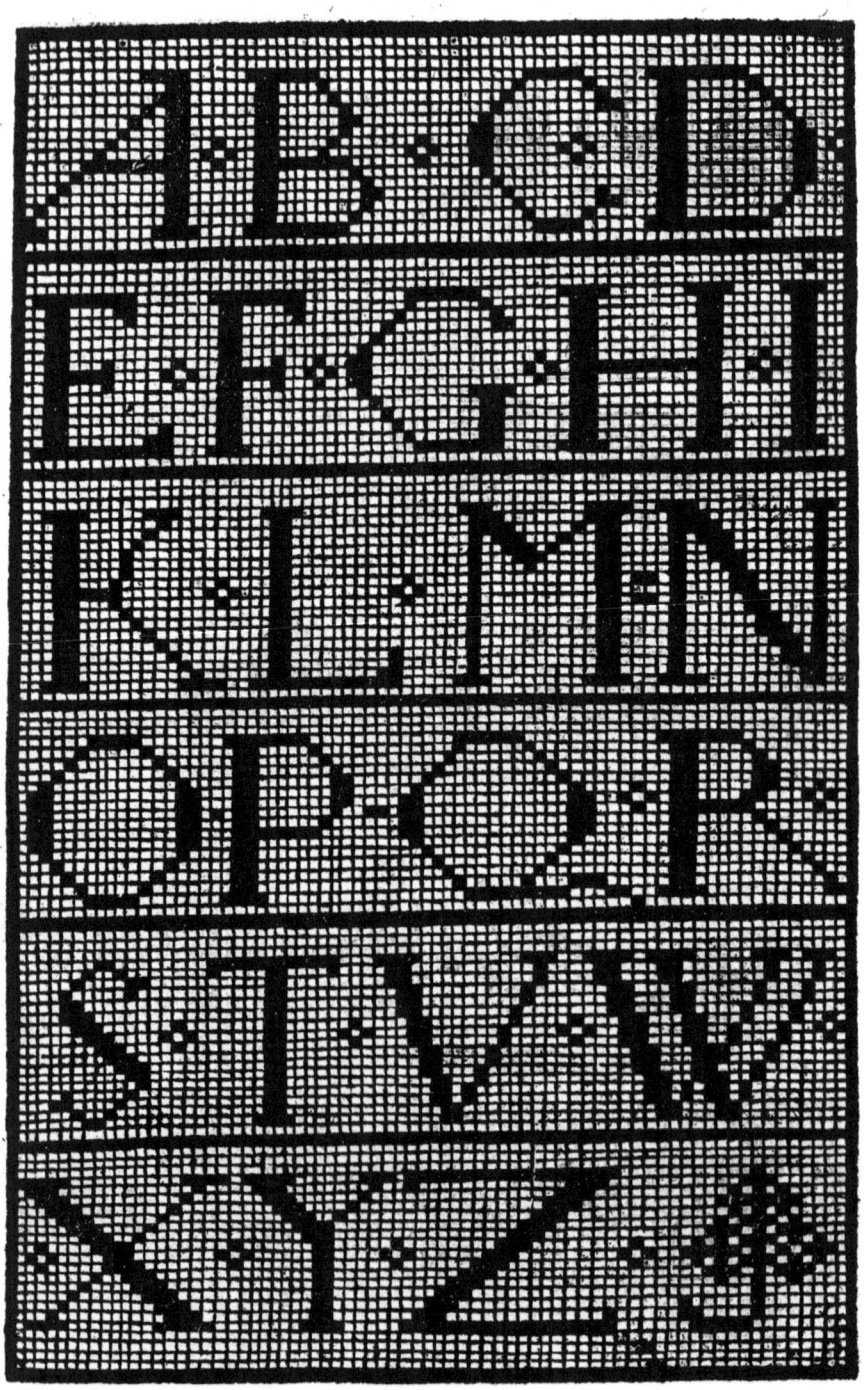

192. Quentel 1544 f.7r

Charted Designs

193. Quentel 1544 f.7v, Gülfferich 1553 f.20v

German Modelbücher 1524 – 1556

194. Quentel 1544 f.9v

Charted Designs

195. Quentel 1544 f.8r

196. Egenolff 1535 f.13r

Charted Designs

197. Egenolff 1535 f.13v

German Modelbücher 1524 – 1556

198. Egenolff 1535 f.14r

Charted Designs

199. *Egenolff 1535 f.14v*

German Modelbücher 1524 – 1556

200. Gülfferich 1553 f.37v

www.ingramcontent.com/pod-product-compliance
Lightning Source LLC
Chambersburg PA
CBHW051544010526
44118CB00022B/2573